EXCEPTIONS TO THE RULES

Redefining Your Path to Success
Beyond the Degree

KENYETTA NESBITT, MBA

EXCEPTIONS TO THE RULES

Copyright © 2022 by Kenyetta Nesbitt

ISBN: 978-0-578-29066-9

All rights reserved. No part of this book may be reproduced, stored in a retrieval system, transmitted in any form or by any means, electronic, mechanical, photocopying or otherwise used in any manner without the prior written permission of the copyright owner.

The information in this book is expressly written from the experiences and perspective of the Author, and all experiences are represented as accurately as possible. The information in this book was correct at the time of publication, but the Author does not assume any liability for loss or damage caused by errors or omissions.

For information regarding special discounts for bulk purchases, please contact hello@simmonshr.com.

www.simmonshr.com

ALL RIGHTS RESERVED
PRINTED IN THE U.S.A.

DEDICATION

To God, my Creator and Father, the sovereign, merciful author and finisher of my faith. You alone deserve the glory and honor for allowing me to have these life experiences and use them as a testimony to help someone else to know how amazing Your love, care, and purpose is for their lives.

To my husband, Dontravious - you've watched me grind and work hard to actualize my God-given dreams. You've supported me, cheered me on, wiped my tears, and stood beside me as I birthed this work of art. Thank you!

To my family – my grandmother Lucille, the matriarch – you raised me, pushed me, provided for me, and ensured I never lost hope in a future brighter than the struggles of our past. I love you and I'm forever indebted to you. It's all for you. Rest in eternal peace.

Mom – I love you. Thank you and here's to a better future!

To my mentees – current and future ones – may you use my life experiences as lessons to help you be better, aim higher, and go further than my feet have ever tread. I believe in you, and I'm always in your corner. My success is your success!

CONTENTS

INTRODUCTION... 2

CHOOSING A CAREER THAT WILL
CHANGE YOUR LIFE...................................... 10

WEIGHING THE COSTS: IS COLLEGE
FOR ME & WHAT ARE MY OPTIONS?.................. 31

THE CURRENCY OF COLLEGE:
FINANCIAL AID 101...................................... 50

CHOOSING A MAJOR IS MAJOR,
BUT YOUR MAJOR ISN'T MAJOR..................... 76

MIND OVER MATTER..................................... 93

IRON SHARPENS IRON................................... 103

THE POWER OF NETWORKING:
DO YOU WANT TO GO FAST OR GO FAR?............ 114

IT'S TIME TO EAT YOUR ELEPHANT.................. 153

INTRODUCTION

May 5, 2018, 9:00 A.M. – I stepped onto the field of Paulson Stadium at Georgia Southern University as one of approximately 2,700 undergraduates eager to witness the conferment of our degrees. It was a radiantly sunny morning. The temperature outside was perfect for a day to commemorate such a momentous milestone. This was it. The moment I had worked so hard for. For the past five and a half years, I had accumulated many long days and sleepless nights writing papers, studying for tests, perfecting research projects, and sometimes, even crying in frustration that getting my degree seemed to be so far away. Some nights, I literally worked myself into a migraine trying to keep my head above water and pass my classes.

The journey had gotten so overwhelming and riddled with seemingly impossible hurdles and challenges to overcome, that I often questioned, "Is this even worth it?" It had been a long, tumultuous journey to get to graduation, but I'd finally made it. Victory was mine! In my mind, the whole thing felt so surreal. It felt like an outer body experience. With anticipation building, I had stayed up until about 1:00 A.M.

the night before decorating my graduation cap with my, then, boss.

As the wee hours of the morning rolled closer and closer to the start of commencement, I still felt weird about the whole experience. Did I really make it to the end? Is this real? What am I going to do when my name is called to receive my degree? Am I going to freeze up in front of thousands of people? Will I trip and fall in these heels trying to get back to my seat? These are some of the questions that filled my mind as I got ready that morning. I had chosen to wear blue as a sign of my loyalty to my soon to be alma mater. As commencement began, my mind became consumed, again, with flashbacks from my journey. I had truly defeated the odds. I had proven so many of the doubters wrong.

After over an hour of name-calling and cheering from the stadium, it was finally my section's turn. I walked nervously, yet proudly to the stage. The announcer completely butchered my name at the last minute despite my spelling out the pronunciation on my name card. As I think back, it was embarrassing, but, in that moment, it didn't matter. With a 3.79 GPA and a recipient of many President's and Dean's List honors under my belt, I'd finally received my bachelor's degree! The ceremony concluded with the traditional release of Freedom the bald eagle to fly around the stadium. Thousands of family members spilled out of the stadium on a quest to find their graduate. In the blink of an eye, it was all over. This chapter of my life was complete.

I'm sure this is a scenario like what you may have heard from a successful graduate or a hopeful student. Even better, my story may sound very familiar to your story if you, too, have carried or are currently carrying the burden of being a college student. You know very well the experience I just described. My experience of academic triumph is unique because I am one of many that society so easily writes off and counts out before I even had a chance to pursue the "American Dream." I am a first-generation college student and graduate, and I am from a rural, underserved community. I am a young, Black woman. I fit the mold of a stereotype. I wasn't supposed to go to college.

My journey was expected to be riddled with teenage pregnancy, bad decisions, dropping out of high-school, and no plans for my future. My story is quite the opposite though. It is because of this stereotype that I became aware of the challenges that beset me. Because of the circumstances and the life experiences I was granted, I knew that I had to pursue the impossible. Many may think college is nowhere near impossible, but, when you've come from where I came from, college can be as rare as affordable healthcare.

Growing up in poverty, it was easy to daydream about what it was like to live better. I spent so much of my childhood wondering why there were little to no opportunities for my family to get out of the negative cycles that haunted us generation after generation. I knew that I didn't want to spend the rest of my life struggling to take care of myself. I knew that my grandmother wanted better for the generations that followed even if it was beyond her means at the time. It was clear that education would be my way of escape. I couldn't just do enough to get by. I had to excel in and outside the classroom.

It was necessary for me to get good grades so that I could, not only graduate high school, but have a good chance at getting into college. My ambition, determination, and perseverance served me well over time as I did just that. I got accepted into college after graduating at the top of my high school class. After the initial excitement wore off, I was left fighting nerve-wracking thoughts and fears that stemmed from being unprepared for transitioning into the collegiate world. After all, I had no one to tell me how to even turn my interest into action let alone get from newly enrolled freshman to successful graduate.

The concept of attending college meant just that - getting in the door. Unfortunately, I did not enter college equipped with the knowledge of overcoming barriers that most families are prepared to deal with simply because I was the first person in my immediate family to even reach the door of opportunity. Many of those barriers included financial challenges, family support, lack of knowledge about resources available within the university, social isolation, guilt, survivor's remorse, and imposter syndrome. As a result, much of my college experience consisted of trial-and-error and learning best practices as I matriculated. I was fortunate to gain a few mentors later in my journey and a praying grandmother whose pride in my future pushed me to succeed.

With each mistake and lesson that I encountered, I realized that my experiences and my voice is needed to illuminate the path for so many other underserved students who need guidance on strategies to, not only survive, but thrive in college and the workplace. This book was written for those, like me, who are eager to actualize all the possibilities that offers, but you are stifled by the tug of war battle between the choice to go to college, whether it's worth it, if a degree will guarantee success, fear of not knowing how to get the most out of your college experience or deciding to scrap it all and build a career starting from the bottom and going up.

Some of you reading this may question what makes my advice so perfect that you should listen to me. There's no way my advice can fit every young professional's situation. Others of you reading this may be thinking you are (or were) not even cut out for college, and you want to go straight into the workplace, so why even waste your time reading this book. Honestly, none of your perspectives are wrong, but I'll tell you why this book will change your life for the better and equip you with tools that are guaranteed to help you clarify your journey to success on your terms.

As I sit here writing this opening chapter, I'm a 25-year-old, first generation, full-time graduate student working on my third degree – an MBA. What's most significant is I've been divinely blessed to have an extensive work history that spans across arenas from corporate America working for Fortune 500 and 1000 companies to working in higher education. Most recently, I've transitioned into higher education, and I've held jobs in various departments that contribute to the knowledge and wisdom I will be sharing in this book.

For example, I've worked in the Office of Financial Aid and been responsible for administering millions of dollars in federal and state funding to eligible students as well as an academic advisor helping students navigate their college experience and tap into campus-wide resources and connections to ensure their success and highest exposure to opportunities. Presently, I am a career advisor who is graced to serve thousands of current students and alumni with identifying their skillsets and career goals, building their career profile, obtaining lucrative career opportunities, and preparing for the workforce. Now, none of those fancy "merits" alone are important; however, those experiences combined with my own challenging, yet rewarding journey through college has graced me with the credibility to share with you all of the spoken and unspoken secrets of maximizing your educational and career experiences.

Because you have chosen to receive this book and receive me, my authenticity, transparency, and honesty, I feel a level of personal responsibility and accountability to help you conquer the obstacles that stand between you and the way you desire to show up in the world. As you dig deep into the content of this book, keep in mind that the views expressed are based on my personal experiences as a student as well as my encounters and lessons learned as a career professional. While this book was written specifically with young, emerging professionals in mind, I am confident there are nuggets of wisdom strategically placed along the way that will provide immense value for anyone of any age, regardless of where you are on your journey to success. In a way, you're like family now, so I invite you to turn the pages with me as I highlight strategies and experiences designed to help you face your future without fear...

TO THE FUTURE...whatever that may look life for you – let's discover it together!

CHOOSING A CAREER THAT WILL CHANGE YOUR LIFE

This chapter is by far one of the most important ones that I have written in this book. Career development is my favorite thing to talk about, and it is so important to me because it has been through the progression of my career that I've discovered who I am, what I enjoy, and how I desire to make an impact on the people and world around me. More amazingly, it has been the vehicle through which I've been able to shatter stereotypes and break generational curses that have held my family back. If you don't receive anything else that is discussed in this book, please frame this chapter, take a picture, post on social media, text or tweet it to your friends, or anything else that will remind you of what we're about to discuss. It is just that serious.

One of the biggest decisions that you will make that will have ripple effects throughout the rest of your life is choosing your career. I want you to understand how big this decision is. Did you know that your career is not as much about you as you think it is? What I mean by that is I firmly believe that we've all been placed here on earth for a reason. Regardless of our race, ethnicity, religion, background, upbringing, and beliefs, I feel we've all been given a unique assignment. That assignment could be a specific location or region, a mass or group of people, a unique cause, a movement, or something else big or small. It should be your mission to seek out whatever your assignment is and work at it with everything in you. Your life experiences and your career are often the vehicle and catalyst to discovering what your life's mission and assignment is and fulfilling it. Certainly, that will evolve and grow into different things throughout the course of your life, but you should be intentional about starting the journey to exploring what that could be as early as possible.

You're probably wondering why this topic comes so early in the book, but you will soon discover that every step you take forward should be influenced by your dreams, goals, and desires for your career. Once you have an interest or an idea for what impact you want to make and what you want your career path to resemble as you grow and mature as a young professional, you can make more informed decisions regarding your educational pursuits, continuous learning opportunities, and the next steps that make the most sense for your career goals.

You can better decipher if it's necessary for you to pursue a traditional 4-year degree and beyond, a 2-year degree or trade, or certifications and trainings to get you going on your path to success on your terms. There's so much that goes into talking about your career goals that we couldn't possibly cover in one chapter of one book, but, in the next few pages, I'm going to do my best to share with you the core strategies you need to know to help you begin planning what your next steps could look like.

Many young professionals don't know exactly what they want to do in their career when they are in their late teens-early 20s. In fact, most of us at that age haven't even begun exploring the world, or ourselves for that matter, and truly living to know the vast options that exist. Up until this point, many of us have lived our lives being instructed on what to do, when to do it, how to do it, and the consequences of not doing "it" by our parents, guardians, family members, elders, teachers, and the like.

Once we reach legal adulthood – 18 in most places – society now, magically, expects us to make our own decisions, know who and what we want to be, and have the A-Z plan on how to be a productive, contributing member of society. Talk about a true contradiction, right? This thought process fails so many of us and causes us to endure costly mistakes that could be avoided or lessened if we have sound strategy to help us navigate this important transitional time in our lives.

If you decide to go to college, you will most likely hear about a Career Center or similar department that offers assistance with helping you identify your career goals, work toward gaining and documenting relevant experience related to those goals and prepare to begin your career post-graduation. They often introduce you to the Career Development Cycle and provide strategies on how you can apply it to your own student experience for a successful career. As I shared with you in the beginning of this book, I am currently in career services, but this chapter was written much later than the Introduction.

I've since gone on to accept a role as a career consultant working in a career center for a large, well-known university, and it's my job to assist students in the aforementioned tasks among many other things related to career development. Therefore, I understand the importance of seeking out and taking advantage of these services; however, there is a growing problem that affects many of us as young professionals. Not everyone has access to this benefit. What if you decided not to go to college? What if you decide to enroll in an online certificate program for a specialized skill? What if you went straight into the workforce after high school? There are many "what-ifs" I could list here to describe every possible path a young professional can take, but regardless of the what if, you still need to know about the career development cycle and how to go about choosing a career path that can change your life positively. So, let's change the narrative right here and right now by talking about the career development cycle and how you might apply it to your life....

Before we dive into the individual stages of the career development cycle, there are a few key points I want to make about it. Most importantly, I want you to remember that the career development cycle is a lifelong process. It's not something you undergo only when you are in your early 20s or just starting out as a young professional in the workforce. It is something that you will continue to experience, whether knowingly or unknowingly, throughout your life. As you learn new skills, pursue higher-paying positions, or even consider switching careers into a different industry, you will progress through stages of the career development cycle over and over again.

It's actually a good thing to actively pursue because it shows a consistent sense of self-awareness and a periodic assessment of your career goals and the trajectory of your career. Are things going as you planned? Do you have the education and skills needed to compete for the jobs you're interested in? Are you becoming stagnant in your career? Are you working in a dead-end job with no chance for growth and promotion? Are you advancing more quickly than you thought? Are you burned out or bored with your current career and want to explore a different career field? Are there new skills you need to develop to get to your desired next level? Undergoing the career development cycle continuously can help provide answers to all of those questions and others that may come up over the course of your career.

Another thing I want you to keep in mind is that there's no one-size-fits-all explanation of the career development cycle. Some interpretations of the career development cycle can be conveyed a little differently depending on the source and where you're getting your information from. Some people may use slightly different phrases to describe the stages of the career development cycle while others may rely on different philosophies to explain the career development cycle. All of this is generally fine as long as you're not being given completely false information that could potentially hurt you more than it helps. You're not expected to be perfect at navigating the career development cycle because there is no right or wrong answer.

It's a matter of identifying who you are, what your goals are, developing an action plan to achieve those goals, and determining what new goals to set. As you learn about each stage of the cycle, don't stop there. I do expect you to do further research in order to help you make more informed decisions. If you received the workbook associated with this book, we'll have the chance to work even more closely together on individual, reflective activities and exercises that will assist you in beginning your own career planning as well as other topics that come later in the book. Now that we're on the same page, let's continue the conversation with the first stage of the career development cycle.

KNOW YOURSELF

The initial stage of the career development cycle is all about you getting to know yourself. During this stage, you should spend considerable time understanding and clarifying your strengths, interests, skills, personality traits, values, and your ambitions. This will help you to form what

I like to call your "Career ID," or career identity. If you have a driver's license or a state-issued ID, then you know that a lot of biographical and demographic information is listed on your ID card, such as your race, height, weight, eye color, address, date of birth, etc. All the information that identifies you as a person.

The same should be true for your Career ID – all the aspects listed above should help you discover who you are and should be determining factors of the type of careers that best align with your traits. You're not expected to know answers to each of the aforementioned aspects off the top of your head. It often requires the assistance of assessments, quizzes, and even conversations with others who know you best to help you decipher who you are. If you've ever heard of a career assessment or personality assessment, this is often what they are used for. There are many assessments and quizzes that exist, and some are free while others have a cost associated with them.

Some common examples of career and personality assessments (in no particular order) include Strong Interest Inventory, Myers-Briggs Type Indicator (MBTI), Enneagram, O*Net Interest Profiler, Clifton Strengths Finder, Holland Code, the Big Five Personality Traits

Model, DiSC, etc. I recommend taking advantage of free and low-cost assessment options. In fact, you can often find a free version of many paid assessments by conducting a simple Google search which will provide the same method of self-assessment as the paid assessment; however, you won't get a lot of in-depth insight and interpretation of your results. If you are interested in a specific assessment instrument that carries a cost, don't be afraid to invest in it.

No matter the route you choose of free vs. paid, each assessment provides very interesting insights that can help guide you in your career development. The important thing to remember with any career or personality assessment you take is there's no right or wrong answers. The results you receive are based on the answers you provide, so you want to answer each question truthfully and honestly based on who you are and how you think.

Now, when I say know your values, I want you to think intrinsically and extrinsically. Not just the superficial, more surface level values you hear people talk about. Think more deeply about what's important to you as a person to be whole, feel meaningful, existential. Beyond that, you've also got to begin thinking about the type of lifestyle you desire to live because that's essentially what your career will support – your lifestyle. Having financial freedom, being able to travel, being able to acquire large assets, etc. Once you have gained the desired insight and discovery of your career identity, you are ready to move into the next stage of the career development cycle: research & exploring your options.

RESEARCH & EXPLORE OPTIONS

Using the wealth of information and insight you've learned about yourself in the first stage, you can now research specific career fields that require and utilize the skills and strengths you possess while also promoting and aligning with your values and interests. I want to take a pause here and stress the importance of self-reflection and exploration because this is a primary way that you can advocate for yourself when job searching for the ideal career that fits you. It's important for you to know what matters to you and what drives the work you choose to do throughout your life.

Knowing this can help you avoid jobs that could make you miserable, unfulfilled, undervalued, and quickly burned out, and identify potential careers that are fulfilling and challenging in a good way. Many people are motivated by money and financial security, so they pursue six-figure salaries. Other values can include accomplishment and recognition, helping others, having variety and change in your work, being respected at work, taking risks, work-life balance, flexibility in work options like being able to work remotely a.k.a. telecommuting, traveling for work, setting your own hours, having autonomy, educational assistance, and more.

Keep this in mind as well as you begin your research and building your list of potential careers. There are a ton of resources available online to help you explore career options across every field and industry that exists. So many, in fact, that it can become overwhelming deciding where to start. Two of my go-to resources that I recommend to anyone exploring career options is utilizing the Occupational Outlook Handbook provided by the U.S. Bureau of Labor Statistics and O*NET Online. Both resources provide in-depth insight, statistics, facts, and growth projections for any industry you can think of.

By exploring each resource, you will find helpful insight, such as median pay, educational requirements, job outlook predictions for the future, and more. Having these statistics can help you decide what educational route is most suitable for your goals. Also, as mentioned earlier, you can begin strategically targeting potential careers that match your interests and skills. In addition to exploring online resources for career research, there are other actions you should take to assist you in narrowing down your list of potential careers and deciding which path you want to plan for and pursue. One of the most important actions is networking.

If you're anything like my younger self, networking may seem like a scary, intimidating thing for you. When I was starting out, I'd frequently heard of networking, and often equated it with wearing fancy suits or work attire in an up-tight corporate environment having to force conversations with strangers or people who are more affluent and well-to-do than I was. I've always had a shy personality, and talking to strangers wasn't something high on my list of fun things to do, so I initially struggled with the idea of networking; however, as I'm writing this piece to you, I can affirm that networking has become a big part of my success as a young professional and a tool that has provided me opportunities to be a part of rooms and conversations with important people and big decision makers, even as a student.

It hasn't been as intimidating or scary as I thought it would be once I'd become self-aware and more confident in who I am and what I want. Maybe, like me, you've heard some people say, "It's not always about what you know, but who you know." That statement can be true depending on your situation or circumstances. On the topic of career research and exploration, networking is a vital tool because connecting with professionals and building professional relationships are essential when job searching or even exploring entrepreneurship.

Networking can help you determine whether a specific career is right for you, learn about industry trends, potential challenges, and opportunities for growth. Research affirms that 80% of jobs are found through networking which is why it's important to begin building professional relationships. A great resource to do so is LinkedIn. With a free LinkedIn account, you can search for professionals based on specific job titles of interest, companies, degree backgrounds, locations, schools attended, etc.

If you're a current college student reading this book, an especially useful feature on LinkedIn is the alumni tool which allows you to search for and connect with alumni who've graduated from the college you're considering or are currently attending. You can even identify and connect with alumni with similar majors or degrees obtained. When connecting with professionals, you can arrange informational interviews which allow you to learn more about their career paths, what it's like to work in your industries of interest, and to build your professional relationships.

Now, for some of us, this may sound like a daunting task to take on. You may be the shy one like I described earlier. Although you're active on other social media platforms with no problem, LinkedIn seems intimidating. No worries, there are other ways to network. I recommend starting with your personal network. Whether you've considered it or not, each one of us has a personal network. Think about it – you may have relatives who currently work in careers that are interesting. Maybe one or some of your friends have relatives who are into intriguing careers. What about past or current teachers or professors, your neighbor(s), someone in your community?

These are connections that you are most likely already familiar with. You have a connection on some level making them somewhat easier to talk to than connecting with a stranger online. Don't be afraid to reach out to them and let them know that you are exploring careers and thinking about your career goals, and you would like to learn more about what they do and what they enjoy most about it. Not only can this help you in your career exploration, but they may have their own personal connections and knowledge of entry-level job opportunities that they could assist you in pursuing. I hope you are beginning to the see importance of networking and how it can affect your career search and goal setting.

While you're networking with people to learn about what they do, careers and industries that are popular, and even researching career paths on your own, one thing that is definitely going to come up is SALARY. While I could spend the rest of this chapter talking about the importance of researching salaries and understanding the power of earning potential, I simply want to stress to you to start researching salaries <u>RIGHT NOW</u>. Wherever you are – preparing to graduate high school, high school graduate, college student, college graduate, in the workforce fully, you name it. Wherever you are in your life right now, it's never too late to learn about salaries.

Use platforms like salary.com, payscale.com, NerdWallet, etc., to search for median salaries associated with the jobs you think you're interested in. You need to know if you'll be able to make a living and get paid your worth BEFORE you dedicate yourself to a specific career. You'll also need to know which career paths have great room for growth and elevation. Understand, I'm not saying that money and salary is everything or the most important thing in life; however, what I am saying is money is a tool. The pay or salary you accept now not only affects your current livelihood, state of paying bills and taking care of your wants and needs, but it also sets the precedent for future earning potential.

My desire for you is have as much information as possible so you can be more confident and well-informed about the career that's right for you. As the old folks say, you can't be out here robbing Peter to pay Paul because you pursued a job that you're "passionate" about, but it doesn't pay the bills or sustain your livelihood and basic needs. You need to understand the significance of a salary! We have to build our confidence around discussing money – that's a whole different conversation for another book but start researching salaries now. Now let's move on to the next stage of the career development cycle: get focused and begin planning.

GET FOCUSED & DEVELOP A PLAN

This stage of the career development cycle is all about developing a clear, strategic plan to guide you in taking action towards obtaining your ideal career. This plan should help you to begin with the end in mind and stay focused. The specific tasks you should complete during this stage include goal setting, decision-making, and defining your plan of action, or better yet, ACTIONS. During the decision-making process, you should utilize the list of potential careers of interest you've developed and evaluate the pros and cons of each career or job title. By doing this, you can initiate the process of elimination to further narrow down your options and prioritize among alternatives. Again, think about the connections between your interests, skills, strengths, personality traits, values, and your careers of interest. Consider the educational requirements and associated financial investments.

You should even be asking yourself specific questions related to your interests and ambitions, such as what's your current life and career situation? Where do you want to be in 1, 3, and 5 years? What are the possible outcomes for each option you're interested in? Which option will get you closest to your desired life and career path? What majors and degree levels are required for your desired career? Are there alternative options besides a traditional college degree to break into your desired career? Are you willing to relocate to pursue your desired career option? Which option(s) will you commit to pursuing? There are certainly dozens of other questions that you can and should consider, but these are foundational questions that often lead to the more in-depth questions.

Once you've begun to make concrete decisions regarding your options, then you can begin establishing SMART career goals (specific | measurable | attainable | relevant | time-bound). Consider what realistic professional goals you want to accomplish in the next 6 months-1 year. If you're a current student, what professional goals do you want to accomplish before you graduate? Do you want to participate in at least one internship or co-op, a study abroad experience, major research project, or volunteer experience? Also, consider what you can begin doing now that will help prepare you for what you may desire to do in the future.

Does it involve pursuing the traditional college route or will taking a certification course or program help advance you? Many people, including myself, didn't have the guidance or had limited knowledge to take time and work through this important step in life. As a result, we've learned through trial and error, costly mistakes, and wasting time in jobs that didn't align with our core skills and strengths nor brought us joy. I urge you to seriously consider this step and develop goals that outline where YOU want to go and what you want to do, not what seems popular or desirable by others outside of yourself. Once you've developed your plan of action and documented your SMART career goals, you're ready to explore the final stage of the career development cycle: taking action.

TAKE ACTION

Although I referred to this stage as the final stage, we've already established the fact that career development is a cycle which is continuous. Therefore, you won't go through this cycle once or twice. Not even three times. The truth is, you're going to encounter this cycle many times throughout your life, especially since statistics show that the average person changes jobs 10-15 times throughout their life. This stage focuses on identifying ways to gain experience in a career field that interests you, navigating the job search process, and connecting with employers.

You should seek out employment opportunities to strategically gain hands-on experience. Depending on your unique situation and circumstances, taking action can look a bit different. If you're a current college student, you should pursue internship and job opportunities related to your major and career field of interest. Other experiential opportunities include volunteer, externships, co-ops, studying abroad, research and class projects, etc.

If you're not currently pursuing college, you can still pursue part-time and full-time jobs or volunteer opportunities to gain necessary experience for your desired career path. The field of Information Technology is booming, and several organizations and companies have developed free (or relatively low cost) training programs to teach you in-demand technical skills. This can be another avenue to consider as a means of building a financially lucrative career.

If, in previous stages, you determined that educational requirements exist for your desired career path, you must weigh your options carefully. We will discuss college and major analysis in the coming chapters, but for now, keep in mind that you want to choose an educational route that aligns with your interests and goals, meets your needs as a young professional, adequately prepares you for the workforce, and is cost-effective to help you avoid taking on extensive financial debt to achieve the necessary educational outcome.

Look at you, on your way to career success! Now you have the foundational strategies you need to begin navigating your dream career path, and it didn't cost you thousands of dollars and you avoided some of the costly mistakes we've talked about so far. As I stated at the beginning of this chapter, do all that you need to do to preserve this information and refer back to it as many times as necessary to help you navigate your future with confidence. If you've read this far, my personal goal has been accomplished. I've shared only a fraction of my greatest lessons, experiences, and knowledge with you, but I can't stop here!

There's more I have to tell you, so take a brief break if you need to – get up and stretch, go grab another cup of your favorite drink and a snack, and let's keep chatting. This conversation gets even better because now we've got a master plan. You know what your ultimate goal is, so now we can work backwards and discuss the process to get there, starting with the pursuit of continuous learning and higher education. Let's go!

Weighing the Costs: Is College for Me? What Are My Options?

One of the biggest decisions that most young professionals will face at some point as you are working to establish yourself and accumulate success on your terms is deciding if college is the right choice for your future goals. This has been a hot debate the past 10-20 years as times and the workforce have changed. There are so many accounts and stories of people who have become successful without ever obtaining a college degree. Many have pursued the entrepreneurship route. Others have opted to get a trade versus a traditional four-year or advanced degree. Others who started college and eventually dropped out.

Some of you reading this may not even be familiar with what the technical term "trade" means which is evidence of my point that times have changed. My goal in writing this chapter is to give you additional important strategies to help you navigate your decision-making when considering whether college is for you, and, if so, to attend a community college or a traditional four-year university. Reflecting on my college experience, I wish that someone would've taken the time to help me explore the options and weigh the benefits and drawbacks of each. Now that I have many years of experience as a student and two degrees (so far) to show for that experience, I can confidently say that I am and always will be an advocate for higher education.

I encourage everyone to take advantage of the opportunity to pursue continuous learning, but there is a mindset shift that needs to take place regarding how we view the college route. My college experience includes attending and graduating from a two-year college and going on to graduate from a four-year university. During my time in high school and even undergrad, going to college was something that was shoved down many students throats as if it was the "one size fits all" solution to becoming successful.

Quite frankly, we have romanticized and excessively glamorized the idea of going to college so much to the point where it's taboo to associate going to a technical/community college or getting a trade with being successful. It's almost as if society has created a class system around higher education attendance where you're somehow seen as better than others if you've attended college and obtained a degree. This excessive glamorizing has put us in a place where millions of professionals, young and old, are saddled with tens of thousands of dollars in debt from pursuing a college degree – many of whom never finished their degree program. Worst of all, many degrees obtained correlate to low paying jobs and an inability to increase their earning potential. Basically, leaving many of us in the workforce that are well educated but struggling financially.

This may sound like a harsh truth initially, but it is reality. The decision to go to college, especially, a four-year university, should be one that is data driven. I talk about this even more in the following chapters, but it has to make sense and CENTS. It's all about strategy and being educated on the financial aspect and obligation as well as the return on investment of the area of study you want to pursue. Simply put, you need to know the facts and statistics surrounding the value of a college degree along with associated costs.

Recall in the last chapter, we discussed researching as a part of your career planning process. In addition to researching career paths, you should also be researching various college majors you may be considering (or currently enrolled in) to determine the average cost of the degree as well as the data around associated career opportunities, average salary, and projected industry growth. These are the nitty gritty facts you need to determine if the decision to pursue said major is going to put you in a position to succeed financially and professionally.

Where society has gone wrong with the "college is the only way" logic is its unfair expectation that 18-20-something-year-olds should know what they want out of life and exactly how to get it. That's where we fail young professionals. That's where I was failed. Being an 18-20-something-year-old is not an age where you are 100% sure of what you want to do with your life, and that's perfectly okay. Choosing to go to college is a life-changing decision, and you need to consider the short-term and long-term consequences. The very last thing you want to do is dedicate years of time, money (DEBT), and hard work to a career that you don't enjoy or are not interested in, only to discover later in life that that was never the direction you wanted to go in.

That's why it's important to explore how your passions and strengths are aligned so that you can pursue them wholeheartedly. Get involved with student and community organizations, classes, seminars, events, and activities that interest you even now. Some people may tell you that you're too young, enjoy where you are, you'll have time to think about that later. Well, I'm here to tell you there's no better time than the present to begin thinking about and planning for your future. Seeking out these experiences as early as possible will help you begin strategizing the best path for you to pursue, and you will be surprised at what you discover about yourself, your interests and what is important to you. Use those experiences as a basis to determine which path to choose for your future.

Many people are afraid to discuss the option of not going to college at all, but I believe that talking about it can you help you make a more well-rounded decision about your future. I have already mentioned that I am for continuous learning, and I understand that there are many paths to advancing your educations as our world has changed. One of the most common is entrepreneurship.

There have been an increasing number of stories of children and teenagers who have become entrepreneurs by using their ideas to create products, services, and organizations which turn into lucrative businesses. There are also many successful entrepreneurs who started businesses in college that became remarkably successful leading them to drop out and pursue full-time entrepreneurship. I support the choice of not attending traditional college if it doesn't align with the career goals you've set for yourself; however, you can't escape having a solid plan, work ethic, and strategy to achieve success by going down a different path. Make no mistake that it will not be easy either way, but having a plan is key.

In being fair and transparent with this conversation, I encourage you to consider other cost-effective education options, such as getting a trade or certificate in a highly specialized area as it can also lead to higher-paying jobs without getting into deep student loan or other financial debt. Another option is self-teaching yourself a lucrative skill – this is quite common when it comes to the tech industry. I know several professionals in my network who've began successful careers in tech simply off of taking advantage of free educational resources like YouTube, Udemy, Codecademy, LinkedIn Learning, etc., or cost-effective training programs.

Some of these platforms may sound foreign to you right now, but I challenge you to go research them. Many professionals have used these resources to teach themselves how to code in different programming languages, build websites, build apps, etc. They've then used this free knowledge to apply for jobs making great salaries. Why? Because in today's world, employers care most about what you can prove you know, not necessarily how you got the knowledge. Reading all of these recommendations probably has you wondering what route to even take. I know, that's why I won't leave you hanging. I strongly encourage you to EXPLORE.

A great option that allows you to get a glimpse into what college is like and creates a strategic advantage in continuing your education is participating in the dual enrollment program. If you're a current college student reading this part of the chapter, then this point is not viable for you, but you can share this nugget to younger people you may know or encounter which would be a huge help for them. If you haven't yet crossed the threshold of high school graduation, this is a golden nugget for you. Dual enrollment is a bridge program offered in many high schools that allows students, usually sophomores, juniors and/or seniors, to enroll in college courses at a local college or university for credit prior to graduating from high school.

This credit will count for both high school and college requirements. If you're thinking this is an amazing opportunity, you are right! There are so many benefits of the dual enrollment program. For one, you get to experience what college-level coursework is like, and you get an early start on exploring potential areas of academic interest. Another great benefit is that the credit you earn by passing those courses will lessen the number of classes and amount of time it takes you to earn a degree. On that same token, you should really aim to pass the courses because those grades become a part of your academic record both in high school and college.

That means that they also affect your GPA before you fully enroll into a college, so you need to take the opportunity seriously if you choose to participate in dual enrollment. It requires an increased amount of responsibility as a high school student in addition to attending your normal classes, participating in sports and student organizations. Although it requires dedication and drive, the results will set you up for success as a full-time college student. If pursued early enough, many students are able to complete an entire Associate degree program by the time they reach high school graduation. I know many young professionals who've done so!

I participated in the dual enrollment program my senior year of high school, and I can't begin to express the impact that it made on my knowledge of the college experience. At the time, the only class options that were being offered at my high school were English 1101 and English 1102 through a local technical college. A year or two after I graduated, the program was expanded to include psychology courses. At this time, the classes were offered in the evenings, so a typical day for me was to drive to school and attend 3 classes during the day. Because I also participated in the work-based learning program, I had a part time job which allowed me to leave school at 11:30AM each day.

I worked for 4-5 hours each day of the week, and I would leave work and drive back to my high school in order to attend the dual enrollment class in the evenings. The class met two times per week for an entire semester. The average dual enrollment course accounts for 3 college credit hours. I know it sounds like a lot, and believe me it was; however, I was immensely proud of the foundation I had set as a result of achieving A's in the program. I started college with a 4.0 GPA and 6 credit hours under my belt. You can do the same as well! I encourage you to connect with your high school's guidance counselor to find out more information about dual enrollment and the opportunities you have available.

Now, let's turn our attention to breaking down the options of community college and traditional universities. Each of them has their own pros and cons that you need to consider. It's no secret that student loan debt is a huge factor against attending college altogether. Choosing to attend a community or technical college versus a university plays a huge role in the debt that may be accumulated. You don't have to let the fear of student loan debt hinder you. In fact, we are going to tackle the topic of financial aid literacy in a later chapter, and I am going to share some strategies to help you maximize your college experience while minimizing the debt as a result. For now, let's continue to dissect the college versus university debate.

I want you to keep in mind that one is not necessarily better than the other, but each offers different advantages based on your goal for attending college, career interests, and preferred learning environment. Also, you'll see where I use the terms "two-year college" and "community college" interchangeably – I'm referring to the same thing. Before we dive in, I want to present a key takeaway that I want you to place in your toolbox and carry with you as you consider the decisions that lie ahead: **BEGIN WITH THE END IN MIND**. By doing this, you can visualize your dream career and how you want to show up in the world and work backwards from that overarching goal into actionable steps and options that are cost-efficient and suitable for you to build a foundation for a lucrative career.

Attending a two-year or community college has many advantages, most notably, a lesser financial burden. As we discussed earlier, costs are one of the number one factors that can influence your decision to attend college. Statistics show that the tuition associated with community colleges are thousands less than public universities and even much less than that of private universities. That is mainly because community college is not structured around offering as many additional amenities and extracurricular experiences and activities that you find at a university. Community college provides a more affordable opportunity to obtain an associate degree or certification in many popular areas, such as nursing, computer science, technology, business, etc.

In fact, there are many career paths that don't require a bachelor's or advanced degree to break into. For example, career paths, such as becoming an electrician, repairman, cosmetologist, dental hygienist, computer technician, etc., can be accomplished by obtaining a trade or certification which is commonly offered at community and technical colleges. If your passions, interests, and gifts make these types of roles intriguing, it may be beneficial cost-wise to consider this path. If your career requires further education, you can easily transition to continuing your studies at a university. Community college also offers a mode of flexibility that is not as common at universities. Most students who attend community college often have many other responsibilities, such as a demanding work schedule, families, etc. One of the biggest benefits of attending a community college is having the ability to take online or evening classes.

Another advantage of community college is that it provides a great transitional experience for students who feel they aren't fully ready for the, sometimes, overwhelming experience of going to a university. After high school, many students are eager about going to college, but remain undecided on factors like what school to attend and what major to study. There is a such thing as being undecided (or undeclared) in your major. We'll discuss this in more detail later, but what I want you to gather from this now is that regardless of what major you choose to study, your first two years or so will be spent obtaining credits for core classes. These core classes are required regardless of your major.

Therefore, if you are undecided about what you want to study, you can still obtain credits for core classes at a two-year college while taking the time to determine the next steps in your educational career. This results in saving time and money that would be wasted as a result of constantly changing majors at a university to find what works best for you. Do keep in mind that you should do your due diligence in researching to determine which (if any) of the college credits offered at a two-year/community college will transfer to your desired university.

A further benefit of the experience provided by a two-year college is the smaller class sizes which increase the interaction and accessibility between you and your professors. During my freshman year of college at Valdosta State University, one of my classes had over 100 students in it. For someone who was extremely shy, I did not feel comfortable at all. I felt very intimidated by being in a class so large. Although the professor was great, I felt out of touch. My experience was much different when I transferred to a two-year college. My classes averaged 35-60 students. My professors were more interactive and available for assistance throughout the class. Having this experience gave me a bit more security and confidence in my path at the time.

Now, let's turn our focus to universities and the benefits that come with choosing this route. College in general offers a unique, important transitional period from teenage years into adulthood. Attending a university widely captures this experience by allowing you to forge many connections, opportunities, engagement, and more. Universities offer expanded amenities that cater to the overall student life experience. There are many avenues by which you can explore your interests, meet new people, discover your passions and values. Because universities are larger, the student body can be more diverse, and the atmosphere is more energetic. With tons of on-campus resources and student organizations, a university campus is always buzzing with things to do and interesting events.

Student organizations range across a variety of themes, including major-based organizations, honor societies, community service, mentoring programs, Greek organizations a.k.a. sororities and fraternities, professional organizations, and more. This atmosphere of student engagement allows you to develop a sense of belonging to something bigger than yourself which can be a life-changing part of your university experience. There are a ton of majors to choose from at universities, and each major is typically housed in its own "college" along with similar majors.

For example, my undergraduate major was psychology, and it was a part of the College of Liberal Arts & Social Sciences along with majors like sociology, anthropology, etc. Most business majors are found in the College of Business. The point I am making is that your college will have resources, events, and assistance available to you that are tailored to your major. This can be extremely helpful as you navigate the university scene. With diverse majors also come diverse classes and subjects. You have a lot more opportunity for experiencing hands-on training and practical curriculum.

Another opportunity that universities offer that is very lucrative and beneficial to students is work study and on-campus jobs. These are paid positions around campus that are typically flexible with your class schedule. The pay is at least minimum wage, but for some jobs, it can be more than minimum wage. Most students will have a job at some point during their college career, and it can be challenging to secure a job off-campus, especially if you don't have reliable transportation or the university is in a city that doesn't have a versatile workforce. Work study and on-campus jobs eliminate this worry. An added advantage is that most students can secure jobs related to their major department. This allows you to gain important transferable skills and experience that will help you to secure a job in your field of interest post-graduation.

My goal in providing this in-depth comparison between community colleges and universities is to offer knowledge that a lot of students don't consider when making such important decisions. This does not eliminate your responsibility to research and gather more information to help you along in the process. In order to make a well-rounded decision, I encourage you to do your due diligence. As I've encouraged before, if you haven't done so already, take some time to really think about your academic interests, your career goals, and what impact you would like to make on society as an adult. Connect with those you know and ask them to share stories about their college experience with you. The information and new perspectives will be invaluable!

With all of this wealth of information, if you're still leaning towards opting out of a traditional college experience, there are other options you can consider and pursue. Depending on your defined interests and career goals, pursuing a certification or trade program may be most beneficial to breaking into your desired career or even entrepreneurship. Certifications are popular across many industries, especially the tech field. We discussed earlier how many professionals begin by self-teaching themselves core skills required to apply for entry-level jobs using various online platforms, resources, and courses. Even if you want to become an entrepreneur, you should pursue educational opportunities and training to increase your knowledge around business management concepts and your area of expertise.

I could fill up the rest of this book with suggestions on different certification, trade, and training programs, learning platforms, and resources, but I'm going to put the ball back in your court and challenge you to begin conducting research into available resources and programs based on your current interests. The goal of this chapter is to bust the myth that traditional college is the only (or the best) way to achieve your career goals and success. As we've discovered, the "best" route to take depends on you and your unique situation and career goals which influence what makes most logical sense to your life. The conversation about college doesn't end here. I want you to have a well-rounded perspective on the aspects of college so that you can make better, more informed decisions no matter if you're a current student or in the stage of contemplating whether college is a good choice for you. Turn the page my friend!

The ₡urrency of College: Financial Aid 101

This chapter is also one of the most critical and essential chapters I've written for you. This topic means so much to me because it has affected me the most as a first-generation college student. It holds the key to experiencing success in most other areas of your college career because if you fall short here, then it hinders you from moving forward. Financial aid is one of the biggest factors that trips students up, especially marginalized students whether you are first-generation or coming from a low-income environment. It's such a complex topic with a million different nooks, crannies, possibilities, rules, and regulations that can be too much for anyone to handle without proper, factual guidance.

Truth be told, many of you may shrug it off as something mom or dad is going to handle so you don't have to worry, but others of you cringe at the thought that mom or dad has no clue where to begin or what to do. I'm equally confident that you or someone you know has experienced some type of financial aid challenge as a college student that forced them to sit out at least one semester or decide to drop out altogether. Unfortunately, there are far too many unfinished degrees that have been smothered due to financial aid challenges. At one point, my college dreams were threatened by it, too, so I understand.

You see, as a first-generation college student, I understood the bare basic idea that financial aid was needed to go to college. I was lucky enough to land a few scholarships from maintaining good grades throughout high school, but that was it. For the most part, I was uninformed about scholarship research except a few sites that seemed like my application would go into a black hole among millions of other students competing for the same scholarships. The FAFSA was familiar to me only because my high school guidance counselor preached that it was necessary in order to get free money from the government to attend school.

That within itself sounded intimidating to me to be honest. I even recall an organized event at my high school where representatives from the Georgia Student Finance Commission talked our heads off about completing the FAFSA in order to receive federal funds. I quickly learned that financial aid was the currency of college and there was no way I, as a poor kid from rural Georgia, could make it without it. Even with all the fancy, positive language and tips preached to me at school, I knew that it was still going to be a challenge because no one in my household even knew what a FAFSA was or how to do it, so it was up to me to figure this thing out with trial and error.

The one thing I did know for sure is that student loans were bad (at least in my mind). I'd heard stories about students racking up student loan debt in the tens of thousands of dollars for a single degree. For many of them, it was debt for a degree that they didn't even use after graduation. I didn't want to get trapped in the debt cycle, so I focused my attention on learning ways to obtain as much free aid as I was eligible for in order to offset my tuition costs. After five and a half years of working toward my bachelor's degree, I tell you that trial and error was an understatement.

Along the way, I experienced turbulent challenges that forced me to have to sit out a semester here and there because there were issues and delays with my FAFSA being processed resulting in me not receiving federal aid, but I didn't let it stop me. I was determined to gain more knowledge on the process and maximize my opportunities each aid year. By the time my senior year came around, I had become what I considered somewhat of an expert on financial aid 101. Thankfully, the day I walked across the stage to receive my degree, I had less than $3,000 in accumulated student loans. The rest of my degree had been paid out of pocket from working a full-time salaried job, scholarships, and grants. I had a rocky journey getting to the end, but I made it. I made many mistakes and took many losses, but I made it without becoming a college debt statistic. I thought my dealings with financial aid ended there, but fate would have it that I would make contact with the world of financial aid again.

I never fathomed my career path would lead me to accepting a job within a financial aid office at an HBCU immediately after graduation. Although I was always good at math, I never had a career goal of working with finances, financial aid, financial awareness, or any field pertaining to money. Yet, there I found myself on the other side of the table now working in financial aid and responsible for administering millions of dollars in federal and state awarded funds to thousands of students, many of whom shared similar characteristics and circumstances as I did – marginalized, first-generation, and a product of an environment plagued by poverty.

It was during that time that I realized that it wasn't so much about what I wanted or was passionate about per se. I was divinely guided and placed into that role to be who I needed as a college student – someone to educate students on how to effectively navigate the currency of college and maximize their attainment of financial aid to overcome the pitfalls that discourage them from fulfilling their higher education dreams. More importantly, I would be equipped with the knowledge and expertise worthy enough to write this chapter of this very book that you are reading today. You may be wondering, how does working in financial aid make me an expert and qualify me to share this knowledge with you?

During my time in financial aid, I gained rigorous certifications from the National Association of Student Financial Aid Administrators in six key financial aid areas including Pell, Cost of Attendance, Direct Loans, the Application Process and Student Eligibility, so you can say I have receipts for this knowledge I'm about to drop. Remember what I said in the beginning - you're like family, and this is a part of my personal responsibility to make sure you have the real, raw facts so that when you put this book down and proceed with your transition, you are ready, and you don't have to depend on anyone to have the answers and do it for you.

You will have some of the necessary knowledge to ensure you, too, become one less student loan debt statistic.

I do want to inform you that the information I am sharing in the remainder of this chapter does not constitute financial aid counseling and it is not intended to take the place of you establishing a relationship and receiving direct assistance from your assigned financial aid counselor or advisor at your current school or the school(s) you're interested in applying to.

The following information is intended for general knowledge purposes and does not guarantee or establish your eligibility for any form of federal or state aid that may be available through a university or college. While my intent is not to serve as your personal financial aid counselor in this book, I do want you to walk away with the knowledge on what this process is so that you can plan accordingly and set your expectations for what awaits you in order to successfully enroll into a college. Now that that disclaimer is out there, let's dive right in!

Scholarships & Grants vs. Loans

A great starting point for this part of our conversation is to discuss the fact that all financial aid is not created equal! This is why it's important to understand the difference between scholarships and grants versus loans. The biggest difference is that scholarships and grants are considered "free" aid in that they are awarded to you, and you do not need to pay them back to the source. Loans involve you borrowing money from a lender, and you are required to repay them whether you complete your degree or not. One of the most important points I want you to take away from this section is that "FREE" IS YOUR FRIEND! If you decide to go to college, be it a two-year college or university, I recommend seeking out and applying for as many grants and scholarships as possible to cover as much of your tuition as possible.

In a perfect world, the goal is to obtain enough grant and scholarship funding to cover all of your tuition each semester. For many people, this has been possible, but it requires investing a lot of time into research and writing essays for a lot of scholarships; however, it can be done with guidance, determination, and persistence. Did you know that there are hundreds of thousands of dollars that students miss out on each year as a result of not applying for scholarships and grants that exist? Also, did you know that there are unique scholarships offered for a variety of experiences, backgrounds, interests, skills, etc.? There are scholarships for minorities, marginalized communities, and other salient identities. There are even quirky scholarships based on things like height.

Seriously, there are so many opportunities to get free money, but many students are uninformed or not willing to put in the effort to pursue these funding opportunities that can help offset the cost of college. My goal is help change that by providing education here and also resources at the end of this book outlining common websites that students can use for free to search for and explore scholarship and grant opportunities to cover the cost of attending college. While the list will be extensive, it is not intended to be exhaustive – you will need to conduct even more research on your own into scholarships available that fit your interests, academic qualifications, background, etc. I got you on the tools, but you've got to be willing to use them to your advantage my friend.

One of the most well-known grants out there is the Federal Pell Grant which is a need-based grant offered by the U.S. Department of Education. This means that your eligibility is based on your financial need. As we've already discussed, this type of award is not required to be paid back; however, your eligibility is dependent on a calculated metric known as the "Expected Family Contribution" or EFC. This unique number is calculated after you submit what's called the Free Application for Federal Student Aid or FAFSA. Don't worry, we'll discuss that in more depth in the next section. For now, though, you need to know that the information you provide about you and your parents' or guardians' educational, financial, and tax situation are largely used to calculate your EFC.

That EFC number is then used to determine how much total Pell grant you're eligible to receive in one academic year. The amounts are set in increments, and the higher your calculated EFC is, the less money you'll be eligible for. There is a certain EFC threshold whereby you may not qualify for any Pell grant funds. The closer your EFC is to 0, the more you become eligible for. At the time of the completion of this book, the maximum Pell grant is $6,494 for the 2021-2022 award year. Be sure to check with the college's financial aid office for the most current Pell grant maximum amount. Most students aren't aware of this, but it's important that you know that that $6,494, or whatever lesser amount you may get awarded, will be split equally between two semesters – generally Fall and Spring semesters.

That means that you will not get the full amount in one semester, so it's necessary that you plan to apply for and obtain as many scholarships and grants as possible to offset the remaining costs that Pell may not cover. Also keep in mind that your eligibility for Pell is re-evaluated each academic year, so you are required to complete a new FAFSA every year in which the amount of Pell you receive can change depending on changes in your family's financial, taxes, and education situation. Now, let's dig a bit more into student loans before we pivot to discussing the FAFSA in more detail.

ALL STUDENT LOANS ARE NOT CREATED EQUAL

We've already established the fact that student loans are contrary to scholarships and grants in that you are financially liable for paying them back to the lender you borrow the money from to support your educational pursuits. If your desire is to attend college at any level (two-year, four-year, trade school, etc.), your goal should be to apply for and obtain as much FREE aid as possible. As I mentioned previously, there are many young professionals who've been able to receive free full rides to college funded by scholarships and grants; however, this may not be attainable for many for one reason or another. In that case, you may decide that you need to pursue a student loan to help cover the cost of college tuition. I want you to be as clear as possible on the stipulations to different types of student loans, so you know what the obligations (and potential consequences) are of borrowing student loans.

First, understand that there are different types of student loans out there. Specifically, you have federal student loans and private loans. The biggest difference between the two is that federal student loans are funded by the U.S. Department of Educations, whereas private loans are not funded by the government, hence the name "private" loans. They are commonly funded by banks, credit unions/credit card companies, state agencies, etc. Under the umbrella of federal student loans exist different categories –

Direct Subsidized federal loans – has a set interest rate, but interest does not accrue (or build up), nor do you have to make payments while you're a currently enrolled student. If you graduate, unenroll from college, or drop your credit hours below what your college deems as "half-time" enrollment, interest will start to accrue, and you must begin repayment of any loans you've borrowed.

Direct Unsubsidized federal loans – has a set interest rate, and interest DOES still accrue (build up) while you're currently enrolled; however, you are not required to start repaying the loans until you graduate, unenroll from college, or drop your credit hours below what your college deems as "half-time" enrollment

Direct Parent PLUS loans – available to your parent or guardian to apply for. Your eligibility depends on the parent's financial and tax income information reported on the FAFSA. Your parent or guardian is responsible for repaying this loan although the funding is administered for your tuition benefit as the student. A credit check is also required as a part of the application process.

Private loans, on the other hand, are even more expensive in the long run to borrow. For example, interest rates are often much higher for these types of loans and are completely controlled by the private lender. Personally, I discourage the pursuit of private loans unless you've exhausted absolutely every other avenue for financial aid. Let's be clear, it's my desire for you to avoid student loans, if at all possible, but I understand everyone's circumstances and family situation are unique. I earnestly ask that you do as much research as possible on student loans to understand the financial obligations you lock yourself (or your parents) into as a result of borrowing them.

There is a huge student loan crisis that has millions of people trapped in a seemingly never-ending cycle of debt. Be aware that excessive student loan debt can be a hindrance for future plans, such as home ownership, purchasing vehicles, and other major assets as they are considered a part of your debt-to-income (DTI) ratio. This phrase is outside the scope of this book, so I won't go into detail about it; however, the biggest takeaway I want you to have from this section is to consult a financial aid counselor as early as possible to understand your options and implications for student loans. Don't be afraid to ask questions! No question is too simple, dumb, or an indicator that "you should already know this." You must do everything you can to make sure you fully understand how student loan debt can affect your life beyond college. You also have to make it make sense for your situation.

I even recommend doing your own independent research FIRST using the federal student aid website linked in the resources section at the end of this book for complete definitions and comparisons between types of student loans and obligations for repayment. Review that website until it becomes committed to your memory – this will help to ensure you're not being blindly influenced by enticing advertisements from lenders and even school officials to get locked into debt that could hold you back for many years to come. It's their job to sell you on these things in order to get customers and students. Your job is to do your due diligence and be able to make a well-informed decision with factual information and statistics. Your future depends on it! Now let's move on to discussing what exactly the FAFSA is – the gatekeeper to federal student aid.

What is the FAFSA? Quick FAFSA facts

The Free Application for Federal Student Aid is administered by the U.S. Department of Education, and you must complete it if you're interested in potentially being awarded any type of federal student aid – Pell grant, federal loans, scholarships, etc. As the name implies, the application can be completed for free online via www.fafsa.gov, and it is a very extensive application including several sections that require you to input information about your educational, financial, and taxes situation as well as your parent(s) or guardian(s) if you're under the age of 24 and unmarried. Again, my goal is not to go into so much depth to the point where I confuse you more than enlighten you, so I'll keep it pretty surface level here. Still, I encourage you to conduct very thorough research and reach out to the financial aid office of the college(s) you're considering for more specific advice and guidance on completing the FAFSA.

The facts that I do want you to take away from this section include understanding that the FAFSA application must be completed each academic year that you're interested in receiving federal student aid for. The application typically opens in October of each year, and schools do a good job of reminding students in the months leading up to the new application opening. It's important that you complete the FAFSA as soon as possible because some forms of student aid and scholarships are time sensitive or limited in funding, so those who complete their FAFSA the earliest often get first dibs on those time-sensitive or limited awards.

The information you enter into the FAFSA will determine if you're considered a dependent or independent student for aid eligibility purposes. If you're categorized as "dependent," it simply means you'll need to provide your parent(s)/guardian(s) financial and tax information to determine your eligibility for federal aid; whereas, if you're deemed "independent," it means that only your financial information (and your spouse's if you're married) is needed to determine your federal aid eligibility. It's equally important to know that most students are classified as "dependent" if they cannot meet very specific circumstances for "independent" status. For a complete list of those circumstances that determine your status, visit www.fafsa.gov. Once your FAFSA is submitted, you will receive a notice indicating that it is processed, and your EFC has been calculated. Again, for specific circumstances surrounding the processing of your FAFSA or any determinations about your EFC, please be sure to reach out to the specific financial aid office of the college(s) you may be interested in.

To wrap up this section, I want to emphasize the importance of sharing accurate, honest information and data on your FAFSA. Being dishonest on your FAFSA can have serious consequences. For many, it may be tempting to underestimate or overestimate information or data, but you don't want to create any issues for yourself that may prevent you from receiving aid due to falsified information about yourself and/or your parent(s)/guardian(s). Many aren't aware about this process until it happens, but the Department of Education implements a process called "verification" each year which randomly flags, or selects, students' FAFSA applications to undergo more extensive scrutiny and review to ensure information and data reported are accurate. This usually requires obtaining supporting documentation from other government entities, such as the IRS, Social Security Administration, courts, etc., to validate the flagged information. Yes, you can get randomly selected for verification despite completing the FAFSA with 100% accuracy, but it shouldn't be an issue for you if you're being honest and accurate from the start.

Beginning with the End in Mind

By now, you've spent quite a bit of time sitting with me and digging into the intricacies of financial aid. I hope I've kept my intent of not confusing you more than helping you so far in this journey. If you're still with me – thank you, friend! If you're a little confused or you've gone down a rabbit hole, take a little bit more time to debrief what you've read so far in this chapter and even couple it with many of the research resources I've highlighted at the end of the book to get a bit more understanding on the gems that I've dropped. Let's wrap up this chapter with one more set of gems that you need to know to make sure you stay ahead of the game if you're considering college and pursuing financial aid to pay for it. Check this out....

Earlier in the book, we discussed the importance of defining and clarifying your why – what are you wanting out of life? What is the lifestyle you envision for yourself? What kind of impact are you seeking to make on others that will lend itself to you attaining a life of abundance, job satisfaction, and maximum career advancement potential? It's based on this self-discovery that you can determine what your end goal is. THIS is the key, friend. In order to get the greatest return from the choices you make – whether to pursue some form of higher education, taking advantage of financial aid opportunities, or launching straight into the workforce – you have to begin with the end in mind.

What kind of degree are you working toward? Undergraduate or graduate degree? How long will it take you to complete said degree? 2 years? 4 years? 5+ years? Are you already part of the way done with your program of study? How many semesters do you have left? Starting with the end in mind and working backwards can help you determine how much aid is needed to complete your degree goals. Not only that, but it helps you to think soberly about the fact that most financial aid sources have a limit before you max out, either on total amount you can receive or total number of years, or not maintaining a GPA over a certain threshold defined by your college's financial aid office. Your goal should be two-fold: 1) DON'T MAX OUT and 2) DON'T LOSE ELIGIBILITY. Let me explain further...

All Decisions Have Consequences (Avoid Major & School-Hopping)

Being undecided in your major is okay to a certain extent; however, it's imperative to not delay the process of discovering the major that aligns best with your career goals and interests simply for the sake of dragging your feet, enjoying the college scene, and the never-ending "I just don't know." I'm not rushing you to make a decision in a split second about a major you may later regret, but you should not be spending the majority of your college career bouncing around from one major to another or hopping from one school to another.

It's tight, but it's right. You may have friends who've done it, but I guarantee if you ask them what they'd change if they could go back in time, they'd likely tell you something pertaining to the major they chose or the time they wasted doing "XYZ" before realizing it wasn't even what they wanted in the long run. I'd much rather you take some time and sit out for a semester or two until you're able to gain knowledge, self-reflection, and insight from professionals in industries of interest and/or mentors to help you make a well-informed decision than to continue down a path that will potentially cause you to max out of financial aid before completing your degree.

Major and/or school-hopping can have not only long-term negative effects on financial aid, but also more immediate effects. For example, a more immediate consequence of switching schools multiple times in the same academic year is that you could very well reach your cap of financial aid budget available for the year based on the amount of financial aid used at previous schools. Why? Some schools are more expensive than others. That means you'll likely be in a bind trying to figure out where else you can get money from to cover any current outstanding balances because you've maxed out your budget for the year. In those instances, and others, I've personally witnessed many students turn to private loans that are not the best options.

As far as more long-term risks of maxing out, you can potentially reach the limit in amount of aid you can receive from Pell, federal student loans, and even state-based aid (HOPE scholarship, for example, if you're in Georgia), if you don't complete your degree in the time frame defined for each aid program. For example, as of the time this book was completed, the maximum lifetime limit for receiving Pell grant funds is about 6 years. Similarly, if you've pursued and received federal loans, the aggregate limit is $31,000 for dependent students and $57,500 for independent students at the undergraduate level. The limit for independent students increases at the graduate level to $138,500.

Federal student loans also have a time limit, even if you don't ever reach the monetary cap. From the time you take out your first loan, you can continue to take out loans for up to 150% of your published program length. That means for a degree program that generally takes 4-years to complete, you are able to receive aid up to $4 \times 1.5 = 6$ years before maxing out. If it takes you longer than that to complete a 4-year program for whatever reason, you will lose aid eligibility. You want to know where I've seen students get tripped up the most when it comes to maxing out? Let me tell you.

Students get caught up the most when they're attempting to switch or bridge from an associate degree program to a bachelor's degree program, or from a bachelor's degree program back to an associate degree program. Because both types of degrees are considered undergraduate degrees, both count toward the lesser amount limit. A university I worked at in the past offered some associate degree programs that had a bachelor's degree bridge program. Whenever I encountered students challenged with the issue of maxing out financially, it was mostly due to them changing their major multiple times, retaking several classes they'd previously failed, or transferring from schools where classes they previously took (that financial aid paid for) didn't count at the new school, so they eventually reached the max time limit or amount limit before finishing their desired program.

I'm sharing this with you, again, so you can be aware of policies and regulations that can threaten your financial balance if you ever run into them. I want to see you win, ultimately, if you decide to pursue the college route as a step toward your future goals. Now, I know you're probably thinking after seeing those amounts that I mentioned earlier, "whoa this is a lot of money" and you might be getting excited to possibly have a lot of bands in your pocket and making it rain but PUMP YOUR BRAKES! The goal is to not borrow more than you need if you truly need loans to cover the cost of college. Getting refund checks used to be popular when I was in school (may still be), but keep in mind that you have to pay every single red cent back to the government (or other loan entities) that you borrow throughout the course of pursuing higher education. It may not matter much in the moment, but when it's time to start the repayment process and you're getting chunks of money taken out of your paycheck, or, even worse, potential wage or tax refund garnishments, it'll be too late to turn back the hands of time.

Don't "F" it Up: Your Grades Can Affect Your Eligibility

The last point I'll make on the ever so extensive topic of financial aid is to make sure you keep your grades up! Your grade point average (or GPA) can affect your financial aid eligibility long before you ever reach a monetary limit or a time limit of maxing out on eligibility. Schools who receive and administer federal financial aid are required to track and incorporate a calculation known Satisfactory Academic Progress (or SAP) as a part of determining your eligibility for federal financial aid – and for some forms of state aid – each semester.

Failure to meet the SAP threshold can put you at risk for financial aid suspension. This threshold may differ from one college to another, but it's important for you to know that this policy exists so that you can do everything in your power to prioritize your academics, maintain passing grades (at least a C or better in most degree programs), and also understand what resources exist on campus for you to seek academic support and intervention as early as possible to avoid failing a class, or classes, and tanking your GPA. That includes the writing center, student success center, tutoring, and other offices around campus that cater to assisting you with academic intervention and resources.

Ending up on SAP (or financial aid) suspension can severely limit your access to federal aid, including any grants, scholarships, or loans, until you're able to increase your GPA back above the SAP minimum threshold. Let me tell you, that is no easy feat. It can take multiple semesters of being on financial aid suspension and making near perfect grades to move the needle in a positive direction toward increasing your GPA once it's plummeted. Is it impossible? No, it's been done by many who've gone before you; however, it is incredibly challenging. SAP suspension can also be triggered by failing to pass at least 67% of cumulative, or total, coursework you've attempted in your program of study, and other stipulations.

As with all other information I've shared for educational purposes in this chapter, I highly recommend inquiring with financial aid staff at the college(s) you may be considering for more specific advice and support based on your individual circumstances. They will be able to put this general guidance into more specific perspective for you. Also, do your own due diligence by researching reputable, trusted government websites (highlighted at the end of this book) – I want you to go into this process with the facts and be as educated as possible on financial aid stipulations, repayment, limits, consequences, etc., so that you can make financially sound decisions that will affect your future beyond college.

Together, we've covered some heavy information in this chapter, but it gets even better in the pages to follow as we round out our chat about pursuing higher education, like choosing a major, and move into the personal aspects of success beyond the degree – dealing with your mindset, building a solid circle, and the keys to networking as you build your net worth. Take a pause, if needed, to gather your thoughts and any notes, then turn the page to continue the conversation....

Choosing a Major is Major, but Your Major Isn't Major

I know you're probably side-eying the name of this chapter like, "What is she talking about? That doesn't make any sense! My major is a big deal…to me. It's what I've always wanted to do. Now she's telling me that what I want and what my passion is isn't important." No worries, I anticipated that your response could be some variation of that. I intentionally titled this chapter in that way for many reasons – **1) It's controversial.** I know some traditionally minded folks or people set in their ways will see the title and be appalled enough to want to read and see what I'm saying because they think I'm too young to even know what I'm talking about.

2) It's a challenge to everything you've ever been taught about going to college, majoring in something you love, going off into the sunset with a 6-figure job and the world being a happy place – which is not as common as you may think. **3) I want you to clearly understand how much the world has changed** and how having a plan and strategy that you use in making a decision about your future is necessary instead of the age-old debate of college is for everyone versus college is a scam – which neither is completely true.

My goal in writing this particular chapter is to continue to expose you to a new way of thinking and challenge tradition by presenting a different perspective. I'll explain exactly what I mean by the title I chose and walk you through the mind of employers and hiring managers, what they are looking for in young professionals, and how a college major plays into it. I sense some of you may be a little hesitant as we move forward but rest assured, friend, I still have your best interest at heart as we continue our conversation.

At the time of writing this particular chapter of the book, I'm six months removed from having completed my third degree, a Master of Business Administration in Human Resource Leadership with a perfect 4.0 GPA (yes, it took me almost 3 years to completely write this book from start to finish). In the beginning of this book, I took you back into time of my graduation day completing my Bachelor of Science in Psychology. The span of time between these degrees is 3 years to date. I'd say with three degrees, I've got the right vantage point to guide you through this chapter. You're in good hands, friend. You got your notebook? Your favorite drink and snack? Alright, let's dive in.

As I've mentioned several times up until this point, it's my intent to educate and enlighten you instead of confusing you. Therefore, I'm going to break this part of our conversation up into two parts. First, let me be clear in saying the decision process involved in choosing a major is VERY important. In chapters 2 and 3, we talked about the journey of identifying a career that will change your life and also determining if college aligns with your goals of creating a life of success, career fit, and impact. This is where choosing a major comes into play.

As much as you may hear people saying they enjoyed their college years, they partied a lot, made many good friends, etc., the truth is that everything about going to college and choosing a major should be seen as a business decision. Does it make good business, financial, and career sense to go to pursue a specific major or school? Ideally, the decisions you make about your career, the desire to pursue college, and choosing a major should yield a great return on investment. Why? Because there are costs associated with each decision. It needs to make CENTS.

This is why it's important to stop romanticizing the idea of choosing a major. I'm sure you've had at least one teacher or professor, family member, neighbor, church member, mentor, etc. rave about choosing a major you love or are passionate about. There's even a decades old saying that goes, "if you're doing what you love, you'll never work a day in your life." Well, that's not completely true either. When it comes to choosing a major, the most effective way to do so is, again, by beginning with the end in mind. Ask yourself, what is your ultimate goal? What career or entrepreneurial endeavors are you interested in? Why those? What educational gaps do you need to fill to pursue those endeavors? What types of jobs can I get with the major I'm interested in? Are they high-paying? What's the total cost of this degree over 4+ years? Will I need loans to pay for it or can I afford it out of pocket?

In what ways can you envision yourself making a difference in your community and the world? What are your skills? Of the skills you possess, which do you enjoy using? What skills will you need to develop or sharpen to attain the type of career or business you're interested in? Many of these questions will require extensive time of self-exploration, research of careers and business ideas, and even activities to develop said skills. For now, I want you to understand that taking the time to reflect and brainstorm on these questions will help you define your end goals.

Notice I said goals, not a destination. Why? Because success isn't a destination, it's a journey. The older you get and the more life experiences you accumulate, the greater understanding you'll hopefully gain about yourself and your purpose. As that happens, your goals will grow, change, take different forms, and become bigger. Choosing a major is not a simple process. Depending on the insights you gain from your self-reflection and the goals you set for yourself, choosing to attend college and choosing a major may be a bit more of a clear cut. For example, if your goal is to become a doctor of some specialization, a lawyer, a dentist, a psychologist/counselor, or other advanced field, then you are most likely going to need not just an undergraduate degree, but you're also going to have to attain an advanced level graduate degree.

These are more common, but certainly not exhaustive. There are various other fields where a combination of undergraduate and graduate level degree attainment may be the requirement to be considered a competitive job seeker. That's why it's important to know where you ultimately want to end up. Ideally, your choice to pursue college and a certain major should be a vehicle that helps you move toward obtaining your goals, not a hindrance, waste of time, money, effort, or resources simply because you just decided to go because others told you to, or you assumed it's what you have to do to succeed.

If you've read this far into the chapter, my hope is that you're reassured that I understand how important the major selection process is. Now let's talk about why your major isn't so major in today's global workforce. Throughout my time working in higher education career services, I've encountered thousands of young professionals who've struggled with the fear that they'll never be able to get their dream job and become successful with their major. They've come into my office as well as my colleagues freaking out about being "doomed" to failure and working menial jobs because their major won't lead to employers chasing them down with job offers.

The truth is young professionals place too much of the responsibility of their success on a major that they discount all of the other experiences they can gain outside of going to class and pursuing a major. A big part of my job in career services has been to help reframe young professionals' minds and bust myths regarding your major and what it dictates about your probability of success. Consider this: your major is only ONE line on your resume. What? MINDBLOWN! Yes, your major takes up only one line on a resume that should be filled with tons of other relevant experiences, skills, qualifications, and accomplishments that help position you as a qualified candidate for the types of jobs you're seeking.

If you don't remember anything else from this chapter, please take away this: your major does NOT equal your career. Ask me how I know. "Kenyetta, how do you know? You have three degrees, so obviously they worked for you." Well first, I speak from experience. When I graduated from high school, I knew that I wanted to go to college and major in psychology because my desire was to help people fix their problems and improve their lives. I had already been developing the personality traits and skills because I was a great listener, observant, and I was always the person in my friend circle who everyone would confide in when having issues and going through tough times. I enjoyed studying the behaviors of others, how we interact with each other as humans, families, friends, and even strangers.

I also really liked learning about the mind, how environments and experiences affect the way we think and view the world, and how our internal biology also affects our cognition. It was a no brainer for me. I knew without a doubt I'd one day become a psychologist, and people would pay me to come lay on my couch so I could listen to their problems, help them find solutions, and make life better. So, what did I do? I enrolled in college and immediately declared my major as psychology. Not one time throughout the 5.5 years it took for me to complete my bachelor's degree did I contemplate changing my major.

Guess what happened in the midst of pursuing a psychology major? I got exposed to several different experiences that ultimately led to me realizing that my calling wasn't to go on to graduate school and become a licensed counselor or psychologist. I got involved in several organizations on campus, I got a job working in the tech field, and several other experiences that expanded my mindset on the endless possibilities that were out there. You may be thinking, "how did you do all of that majoring in psychology?" That's just it - my experiences were teaching me that although my major at the time aligned with what my goals were, the things I got exposed to outside of the classroom shifted my mind to see that my major didn't equal my career. By the time I finished my psychology degree, I was working for a tech company as a software applications specialist and project coordinator, and I was (and still am) highly successful.

Do I regret ever pursuing a degree in psychology? Absolutely not because it was through that program of study that I learned several skills, qualities, and competencies that I still use every day in my personal and professional life despite not being a psychologist or counselor. I've learned important interpersonal skills, I've been professionally trained on cognitive disorders, mental disparities, and other factors that influence the way people think, behave, interact with others, live and work. I've been able to apply a lot of concepts to being a leader, managing people, and understanding organizational development. That's really what it's all about. If you hang your hopes on going to college, pursuing a major and expecting that degree alone to guarantee you success, then you're setting yourself up for imminent failure.

A major or degree alone can't do it. IF you decide to go to college or are currently enrolled, you must be strategic in how you make the most of your college experience and the development opportunities you seek out. You can maximize your return on investment there by networking, taking elective classes that will teach you transferable skills that can be applied across different career fields, such as business classes - finance, marketing, organizational development, accounting, etc., computer science-related classes, and more. Get involved with organizations that not only align with your academic interests but also professional interests where you can network with other professionals across different industries, participate in conferences, competitions, etc.

Study abroad, travel, volunteer in the community, develop core competencies, like emotional intelligence, public speaking and communication skills, problem solving, analytical skills, and even enhance your understanding of the art of effective business communication. All of these experiences take place outside of the classroom. Going to college can't just be about pursuing a major, taking the required classes, and graduating in a few years. Think holistically and creatively about what you can do to help maximize your possibilities for success. After all, you're paying for it, so it makes the most business sense to take advantage of as many opportunities afforded to you.

Secondly, there are millions of professionals around the world who are enjoying successful careers that are nowhere near related to the major or degree they pursued or obtained in college. MILLIONS. That's the power of networking, which we'll discuss in more depth in the pages to follow. I will be teaching you some foundational tips to start networking with others because it is through these conversations that you will hear firsthand from successful people working in a career you may be interested in, that majored in one thing, but their career involves doing something totally different. I see it every day working in career services. EVERY DAY. People who major in one thing and end up pivoting to do something different, and it's through the transferable skills that they've gained that allows them to do so.

Let me tell you that I work with employers across every industry you can think of, including Fortune 500 and 1000 companies, who focus their hiring efforts on experience and skills instead of degrees alone. In fact, workforce development trends are showing the same thing! The workforce as we know it has changed drastically. As I've said in a previous chapter, there are so many learning platforms available on the internet, like YouTube, Udemy,

LinkedIn Learning, etc., where people self-teach themselves several in-demand skills like tech skills, programming languages, emerging technology, marketing, graphic design, etc., that allow them to successfully break into fields where a decade ago, you'd probably need a degree for a recruiter to even blink at your resume. You even have companies like Google and Microsoft who've created their own educational platforms and learning academies to teach you relevant technical skills and then hire you into a bootcamp or program to ultimately get a job with them.

I see it every day, I have several friends who've successfully done this. I, myself, have done this! There are several certificate programs out there, too, that equip you with skills across different career fields that employers sometimes value more highly than a degree, especially in the tech field. Now, am I saying that college is a waste and that you can learn everything online that a degree can teach you? ABSOLUTELY NOT! Remember, I have three degrees myself, and I don't regret pursuing any of them. Actually, if I could go back in time, I would adopt a slightly different strategy to maximize each degree even more.

I'm simply conveying the importance of understanding that you can't lean solely on a major or degree, blindly thinking it will guarantee you the great paying job you're dreaming of or the successful career you deserve. In today's workforce, you're competing against people at all levels, those with and without a degree. You owe yourself the best return on investment by maximizing your selected major if you're heading down the college route. In fact, what you devote your time and interests in outside of the classroom should complement and enhance what you're learning in the classroom.

Allow me to share one final experience that I hope will drive home the significance of what we've been chatting about in this chapter. When I began my MBA program, I was navigating such a weird landscape. You see, there wasn't a time before now that I thought I had an interest in pursuing a business degree, and I knew that the career opportunities that are available for someone with a background in a business discipline were so vast. Because I believe in practicing what I preach, I wouldn't encourage you to seek out mentors and network with others to learn about specific career fields and how to successfully pivot into your dream career without applying the same principle to my own journey.

I remember being about a year into my program when I decided to deep dive into a search on LinkedIn for MBA professionals who were thriving in the human resources industry. Through self-reflection, discovery, and clarity, I'd been able to narrow down how well human resources aligned with my initial goals for pursuing a psychology degree. Remember, I've always wanted to work with people and help solve their problems. Well, the more I learned about myself and the more experiences I gained through the years, I realized that that translated into helping people unlock their potential, obtain and maintain meaningful careers.

As a result of extensive time spent searching on LinkedIn, I came across many people whose profiles were very interesting and the types of jobs they'd held were similar to jobs I'd thought about pursuing myself. I sent them all connection requests with a brief note introducing myself and inviting them to chat briefly about their background and any tips they could provide to a current student looking to break into the human resources industry. While most of them accepted my connection request, I recall only one or two of them responding to my message agreeing to speak with me about their experiences growing their career.

One of them in particular happened to be someone in a senior leadership role in HR. He also happened to have completed an MBA degree about 15 years prior to the time we connected. Fast forward to finally scheduling a chat with him, we were discussing his background, his journey navigating college and building a successful career. Throughout the conversation, he'd shared valuable gems and nuggets of wisdom regarding things to be on the lookout for, how to maximize my degree, the importance of networking where I am, and presenting myself as a sponge willing to soak up as much as possible about my field of interest.

There was one piece of advice he shared, in particular, that struck me and still sticks with me to this day. He said that whether I believed it or not, a few years from now, my MBA won't matter. His doesn't matter 15 years later. Why? Because of the advancement of technology and the world of work, the concepts taught in his MBA program 15 years ago, let alone in my MBA program today, will become obsolete. He further explained that the perceived "clout" of having an MBA loses value really quickly when you're competing in a global market with professionals around the world. Further, he recommended that if I wanted to continue to reap the benefits of an MBA, that I should always maintain my desire to be a continuous learner – to never be afraid to be in rooms with people whose intelligence, strategy, vision, and network were larger and more advanced than mine.

It's in those rooms where knowledge is being shared that can help you get to the next level, as long as you're willing to learn and not be so quick to throw your credentials around as if they make you more valuable than the next. In fact, most people who are thought leaders, decision makers, movers and shakers, are qualified in their own right. If you want to become like them or rise above them, you must be willing to learn from them – especially mistakes. Again, this is why your major alone cannot be your only source of hope for obtaining the success you seek.

With this new knowledge imparted, I hope that you feel more confident and clearer on how to blaze the best path for yourself if your end goal influences you to pursue college at any level. Knowing how to utilize your major to maximize your return on investment is an avenue for getting to your definition of success, but your mindset, character, integrity, and your circle of influence will help to keep you there. As we transition to the concluding section of this book, we'll wrap up our time together by discussing the "you" behind your success. See you on the next page, friend!

Mind Over Matter

Dealing with the Mental Pressures of Carrying Your Future

Adulthood is like a whole new world for young professionals who have reached their rite of passage through graduating high school. For most people, your high school career is marked by great adventures, fun times, your first car, your first job, and even more "firsts." Everything in your life so far has been familiar and exciting, but adulthood is totally different. If you're not careful, the intimidation and, sometimes, ambiguity of being in college or in the real world of the workforce can really swallow you and stifle you from even pursuing your educational goals.

I can't stress how much this time is very important for you to really reflect on who you are, your values, and your intrinsic motivation. You must analyze all the internal and external factors that you will carry with you into your first day on campus as well as the ones you will meet while there. One of the most important things you must conquer is your self-awareness and having the right mindset. If you are a first-generation student, you know very well the struggles and isolation that sets in when you are the first in your family to do anything. You feel like you must accomplish whatever your goal is because you will be the one to save your family and change the way you live and experience life. Mama didn't do it. Daddy wasn't around. Grandma put her educational and career pursuits on hold to take care of the family. Cousins, aunts, and uncles couldn't seem to do it either. Therefore, you must be the one. I understand it because I have lived it and I AM living it. After years of hard work, you do become that one who accomplishes the goal of making it to college, but what about those feelings that set in afterwards?

There will come a time where you will be faced with negative thoughts that attempt to guilt you into feeling bad for being the only one who made it. I like to call it "survivor's remorse." You see, psychologists have coined the phenomenon "survivor's guilt" to refer to a mental disparity where survivors of a tragic event feel guilty or that they have done something wrong when they survived, but others did not. They often question themselves or things they could've done differently. My idea of survivor's remorse stems from that, except, we often ask ourselves, "how can I accomplish this, but my family is still suffering and struggling?"

We may even convince ourselves that we don't deserve the opportunity for whatever reason. We're not capable, don't have the skills or "smarts" to even be in college or to obtain a specific job. Better use of our time can be spent working extra hours and shifts to help pay the bills and keep food on the table. This is known as imposter's syndrome. Let me tell you that this pattern of negative thinking and self-talk will only hinder you from truly embracing your opportunity to experience all that a successful college experience or career has to offer you. You DO deserve to be where you are. You worked hard to defeat the odds. You put in the time and effort to reach this milestone, and it is okay for you to walk into the door of opportunity boldly and confidently.

Know that your past doesn't determine your future. Things that happened to you or around you that were beyond your control are only experiences that have shaped you into a resilient person who is more than capable of continued success. More than you have proven to others, you have proven to yourself that you can do anything that you set in your mind to do. Will it be perfectly executed without mistakes? Does it make you incompetent? No, of course not! No accomplished person has achieved their level of success flawlessly and without failures or scars. You must remember that it all ends with YOU. The lack, generational curses, stereotypes, and poverty. You can eradicate what your ancestors had to suffer through. You have the power to change the trajectory of your family's livelihood for future generations because of your decision to pursue a path to better which may or may not include formal higher education.

With the decision to pursue higher education or building your career comes increased pressure to do well and succeed. Along with the pressure of being the first to attend college in some cases, it may also feel like you've adopted the burden of being a role model for younger siblings or family members that are following in your footsteps. I know it's a lot to bare, but you should allow that confirmation to fuel you and not scare you. You're a life-changer! Navigating the rollercoaster of college and architecting your career by seemingly starting from the bottom is going to test you in many areas. In fact, one of the biggest things that will be challenged is your identity, especially if you are a first-generation student, or you've come from a marginalized background.

Society has already tried to associate your identity with the stereotypes that come with being a "first-gen" student. Others may perceive you as not willing to work as hard, or they will expect you to give up because you don't have a lot of the answers. Stop right here in this moment and really focus on what I'm about to say: "first generation student" is only a classification. It is not your sole identity, and it does not define your capabilities. Don't allow anyone to define your identity for you just because you are classified as a first-generation student or any other marginalized aspect. That can predict nothing about your ability to succeed or the impact you will have on the world.

In order to truly be able to experience the feeling of success in being in college or in a career, you must learn how to manage your expectations. That includes taking on the expectations of others, especially your family, peers, and coworkers. You are not your family's wants, anticipations, or dreams. You are your own! You must be careful not to allow your family or friends to make you doubt the decisions you make about your journey. Of course, you want their support and assistance as you take on this new chapter of your life, but it will be important to be firm about your decisions, especially if you've received trusted, vetted guidance or mentoring and have weighed all options and consequences.

One of the best pieces of advice I was given as a first-generation student is to not allow people to project their fears onto you. What happened to them and around them is not an indicator that it will happen to you. While family members and friends often have good intentions, sometimes those good intentions are backed by fear. One thing you'll learn as my newfound friend is that we cannot and will not operate based on fear. We operate in facts, research, and most of all faith and trust that we have a purpose to fulfill. It won't be an easy thing to transform your mindset because it may feel, for some of you reading this, as if you have been in survival mode for much of your life.

You've been so focused on the daily grind of going to school, and, for some of you, having a job to help support yourself and your family. It's okay. It will be a daily process. You will have to develop routines, such as reciting affirmations and focusing on the positives. I recommend journaling as a form of personal motivation and encouragement. Write about your accomplishments as well as the feelings and emotions you associate with them. That way, when you begin to face moments of uncertainty or scrutiny from others, you can revisit your writing to refresh yourself and continue to motivate yourself to keep going. Consistently celebrate yourself for how far you've come and even the small daily victories. Trust me, cheering yourself on is a necessary part of building the foundation for your support system that you will need in order to remain balanced as you forge ahead into your path to success on your terms.

Whatever your life's circumstances have been up to this point, it can be very easy to talk yourself out of a life-changing opportunity simply out of fear of stepping into unknown territory. That's why when preparing to embrace any type of change in life, it's most beneficial to ensure you maintain a mental and emotional balance. Explore your feelings and emotions. If you're feeling scared, explore the root of that. Why are you scared? Is it fear that you're going to fail and be embarrassed? Is it because of someone deflecting their beliefs and fears onto you about negative outcomes of your change? Is it because of the unknown of what may exist on the other side of your transition? You must become aware of your inner thoughts because overthinking is like quicksand.

The deeper you allow negative self-defeating thoughts to dive, the deeper your fear becomes of the transition to something that has the potential to change your life for the better. You must also set realistic expectations about the process of your transition. You can't be too hard on your yourself or expect to have the answers to everything. College and the workplace are both two gigantic worlds that aren't meant to be navigated alone. An effective way to pace yourself is by setting expectations for tasks that must be accomplished, etc., but be flexible with the flow of each day. This will be extremely important as you take on the admissions process, searching for the right college for you, and even beginning the job search for your career.

Perhaps the most significant piece to preparing for transition is understanding your why. This will be what keeps you grounded and focused when you want to abandon the process of change or allow fear to get in the driver's seat. Your WHY is what fuels you when you feel you can't go any further and nothing is working. That inner fire that lights the path between where you are now and where you're destined to be if you don't give up. Your why will help to feed your faith. Les Brown, one of the world's greatest motivational coaches and speakers, reminds us to, "feed your faith and your doubt will starve to death." What you feed will grow, so feeding your why will produce a harvest of abundance and success.

I must also remind you, don't be afraid to identify role models and people who inspire you. They can be famous or even local people whose impact you resonate with. For me, I've always admired other African American women who have come from similar backgrounds and experiences and were able to build a successful life despite where they came from. One of my biggest role models is the former First Lady of the United States, Michelle Obama. I hope to be able to meet and work with her in person one day and get her to autograph my book "Becoming." I also admire Tyler Perry's story.

Whatever role model you choose to be inspired by, always remember that where you come from does not decide where you can go. With the proper mindset and preparation, the possibilities of success are endless! Remember, though, that the level of success you desire and dream of can't be achieved alone. You will need accountability and a trusted circle of people who can help you stay focused and on track to accomplishing your dreams. That's where we'll turn our attention next. The significance of a support system and how to cultivate one that's effective for you. See you in the next chapter!

Iron Sharpens Iron

Building a Solid Support System

Everything you need to be who you've been destined to be is already inside of you. It just requires the right people to help cultivate and nurture it. That's why having a solid support system is key to achieving the level of success you desire to reach. More than you need a six-figure salary, famous career, or notoriety, you need to be connected with people who've been down the path you're dreaming of pursuing and who can help guide and mentor you to avoid the pitfalls, scars, setbacks, and setups they encountered. Experiencing trials is an inevitable part of life. Going to college or launching a rising career are two phases in our lives where trials seem to hit us repetitively and intensely.

Stress and frustrations, sometimes, build to an all-time high. You experience stressors from, seemingly, every direction – the pressure to fit in to specific social circles, consistent class attendance, homework, extracurriculars, student organizations, working, passing classes, managing your finances, home life, dating, relationships, building a career, learning workplace politics just to be respected in the workplace, and the list goes on. It's challenging to juggle all of this and maintain your sanity and strength. It's practically impossible to go at it alone. At the core of our human existence is the need for interaction and support. In fact, you should have the expectation and desire for support from those around you, especially your family and friends. The overarching goal of having a support system is to maintain accountability, decrease stress, and having others to do life with. We all want people around us who will listen and give feedback; who will be a shoulder to lean on during tough times; and who will help us to stay focused on the road ahead of us. There will be several moments as a young professional where you will get depleted. Your level of frustration will be so intense that you will want to give up and throw in the towel. Therefore, having a support system is vital to your success.

Your support system will be your primary source of accountability when you want to give up. They should remind you of what you set out to do, especially during the moments where your judgment is clouded by the difficulties that seem to corner you. They can serve, primarily, as your buffer against disparaging times which can lead to feelings of depression and anxiety. As a first-generation student and young professional, I know it can be a lonely road when you're trying to do something that's never been done. Although I knew I had the support from my family, I often avoided confiding in them when I was experiencing hardships because I felt like they wouldn't understand my frustrations. As a result, I suppressed a lot of my feelings and emotions which often made it more difficult to overcome challenges. That's why it is necessary to not only have that circle of support, but also be willing to let them in.

When I first went off to college, my expectations were placed entirely on my family to be my circle of support. Leaving high school, I had a small group of friends. That worked well until I made the transition to college. When I started getting hit with various challenges and setbacks, I often felt disappointed and frustrated when my family couldn't help to alleviate the problem. It was in those moments that I learned very quickly that my expectations were too extreme in that I could not rely solely on my family to be that place of solace and refuge. Of course, I knew that my family would always be there for me, but I also had to manage my expectations as to the extent of how they could be there for me.

As a young professional, and especially first-generation student, you must identify and accept the very real fact that your family wants to support you (in most cases), but sometimes, they may not know how, especially if the situation or experience is totally new to them, too. Consider this, your family is taking on a new journey as well. Therefore, this period in your life is critical for them as well. Be a bit flexible in your expectations until everyone can adjust to your new reality.

For those who decide to go, most students arrive to college with a large network of friends and connections, but the reality is, college will show you who your true friends are, and it will also redefine and reshape your level of connection with existing friends and newfound friends. As your college experience begins to take shape and evolve, you may decide that you need a large network of support, or, in some cases, a small, more intimate support network.

It's important to remember that no matter what size your support system is, you don't want to limit it to only certain kinds of people. More specifically, your support system can be family, friends, church members, fellow classmates, professors, mentors, neighbors, dorm roommates, etc. Once you become involved on campus, you may discover organizations that become like a second family and pillar of support for you. Variety and diversity within your network are the goal! It may seem a bit intimidating at first to try and make connections with other students, some who have come from different walks of life that are completely different from yours. Therefore, you must consistently reassure yourself that members of your support system may not look like you, but that's okay.

On the other hand, when you're on the rise in the workplace, a key ingredient to your success is, not necessarily focusing on being liked by everyone you come into contact with but positioning yourself as a team member who contributes value, developing great professional relationships, and forming allies that can support you in growing your career and gaining access to rooms you otherwise wouldn't be able to tap into. A part of that is accepting that all of your allies may not look like you, and that's fine.

Does that mean you need to always be smiling in everyone's face and going to work just to make friends? Absolutely not, however, you should strive to have positive interactions and build a positive rapport with everyone you meet while, respectfully, developing and exerting boundaries that protect your peace and you from being devalued or mistreated. As I mentioned earlier, just about every workplace you encounter throughout your career will have some level of workplace politics. It's just the games people play. Depending on the industry and type of job it is, the politics are much more intense than in other places. It's important to learn how to play the game without compromising your integrity.

One of the most important things you should pay attention to when building a support system and key relationships is people's personality and the energy that they carry which leads me to the most important topic of this chapter: determine who is healthy and who is TOXIC to your peace and overall wellbeing. The last thing you need is someone in your space who constantly adds to your stress, frustration, and the overall decline of your self-care. To combat that, I encourage you to begin taking inventory of the different personalities that are already within your network. Make a list of people if necessary. Evaluate whether they are generally positive or negative in nature.

Do they motivate you and encourage you, or do they constantly talk down on you and your circumstances? Even if they don't talk down on you, are they negative in general? Is their language one that always speaks to build people up, or are they always complaining and dragging themselves and others down? Do they uplift you and push you closer toward your goals, or do they dissuade you from whatever it is you are trying to pursue? Do they influence you to partake in experiences that will enhance your success or experiences that will inhibit your success? Do they carry themselves in a way that shows they are also diligent about accomplishing goals that move the needle toward success, or do they squander time every day involved in meaningless activities that won't yield any success? You need to limit as much negativity and complacency as possible. Negative people will serve to only bring you down and create more strain.

I cannot stress enough how impactful it is to have the right people around you as you embark on this new phase of your life. Studies show that positive, reciprocal relationships can lead to a greater overall wellbeing, a more stable emotional and mental state, more enhanced coping skills, and an increased sense of self. Remember that support can be shown in many forms, such as emotional, physical, mental, and financial. In order to reap the true benefits of support, you must be willing to ask for help and be receptive to it. You will truly recognize its significance as you become more susceptible to distractions.

Power Circle: The Importance of Like Minds

It is my hope that as your transition begins to take shape, that you lend your focus to building a power circle of support. Within this power circle should exist personalities who are like-minded in the sense that your goals are to figure out who you are and what your gifts and talents are to be shared with this world. Should each and every one of the people in your circle think exactly the same? Absolutely not! By like-minded, I mean everyone should have some goals established, a plan they're working, and strategy for building their lives.

It's important to accumulate a circle of forward thinkers and movers; trusted allies who want to take action, execute and build momentum both in school and in their careers. You must build your circle by attracting people who will hold you accountable to your dreams and the calling on your life. Now, this isn't some BFF, bestie type of situation. Sometimes, the going will get tough, and you won't agree with everything your power circle thinks or does, but if there is authenticity, love, and commitment to seeing each other succeed, they'll have your back and push you when you don't even have the strength to push yourself.

You may have heard the quote, "you're the sum of the 5 closest people around you," or "if you show me your friends, I'll show you your future." While the intent of those quotes is to get you to deeply examine who you spend most of your time with, I believe we're all influenced by a network of people beyond the 5 people who we feel we're the closest to. Especially since we live in a world that is so connected by social media and the constant need to be seen, posting, getting likes/reactions, etc. My goal is for you to increase your intentionality in who you choose to be in connection with and who you choose to allow in your sacred space to have influence over your now and your next.

How Round Is Your Circle?

If you're thinking like me, you may be wondering, "how round is your circle?" I don't mean that to be funny or petty (I admit I did laugh a bit as I wrote it), but seriously speaking, you must continuously evaluate how round your circle is. If you're at least as old as I am, or older, you may remember going to the doctor's office as a kid. If your doctor's office was anything like the ones I've encountered, there were often fun, interactive toys and contraptions that awaited young kids as an effort to keep them occupied and behaving while waiting to be seen. I vividly remember one of the many toys available happened to be a wooden puzzle with large pieces. Each piece usually had different shapes, colors, or words that matched a specific space within the puzzle. Of course, you know that in order to put the puzzle together completely, each piece had to be fitted perfectly in its *right* spot. Putting a piece in the wrong spot could jeopardize the puzzle because it wouldn't allow for other pieces to fit properly, and you wouldn't be able to see the finished masterpiece.

The same idea holds true for your power circle. You can't have the wrong pieces (people) in the wrong places. Truthfully, you can't even afford to have the right people in the wrong places. So, as we wrap up this chapter, I encourage you to begin taking inventory of your circle. Who are you including? What are the qualities and characteristics that you desire to have in the people that are in your power circle? Are those qualities ones that will help you become a better person and help push you towards your best? Of course, this can't just be an outwardly judgment. You must also look inwardly at yourself. You must also devote some time to inner work. Do your personal qualities and characteristics warrant a strong circle? Do you give as much support and accountability to members of your circle that you expect to receive from them? The most powerful circles are ones where actions, accountability and support are reciprocal. Now that we are clear on the importance of developing your inner network of support, let's turn our focus to the importance of networking to build connections in the outside world. After all, your network does influence your net worth!

The Power of Networking: Do You Want to Go Fast or Go Far?

Those who know me know that I'm a person who loves affirmations and phrases that help me to cast big vision. Not just big vision, but also helps to remind me of my path to purpose and progress towards success. One of my favorite adages that is popular, yet often undervalued, is an African proverb that states, "If you want to go fast, go alone. If you want to go far, go together." It may be a saying you've heard before, but its value can often be discounted by some people who quote it. Sure, at surface level, we can understand the saying is basically telling you that in order to go far, you can't do it alone; however, this saying manifests itself truly when it comes to the idea of networking. Networking is something that is heavily slept on by a lot of people for so many reasons. I was one of those people who never really tapped into the true power of networking until recent years.

I've shared with you my experiences of excelling throughout school, making connections, building a career, etc., and I'm sure you're probably thinking "duh, you have to network to accomplish all those things. What's your point?" My point is, those experiences, while valuable and proud moments, only struck the surface of the power of networking for me. There are so many opportunities in life that can only be actualized through building strategic relationships as a result of networking. It doesn't matter if you have a dozen college degrees or never step foot into another school after high school. Networking is the major key to building wealth, growing your career, getting into important rooms, and expanding your sphere of influence regardless of what it is you are skilled to do. As the young people say these days, "shooting your shot." Networking is about shooting your shot with people who have information or access to resources, places, and other people that can help you move the needle toward the success you seek.

The older you get and the more people you encounter in academic or professional spaces, the more you're going to hear people rant and rave about how your "network equals your net worth." What does that really mean, though? For many people, the thought of striking up conversations with a complete stranger is often uncomfortable, intimidating, and scary. Others severely discount networking to something that well-known, rich, successful, well-to-do people do. They imagine it being a room full of people in fancy suits with important titles – CEO, COO, Vice

President, etc., mingling. While that can be true in some circumstances, authentic networking in today's world is so creative and diverse. A lot of it happens online, from the comfort of your mobile phone or laptop, as well as in-person.

My whole purpose in even dedicating a chapter to networking is because it is a strategy, that if implemented effectively, can be a catalyst to you achieving your definition of success whether you've decided to pursue college, growing your career, or building a business and, ultimately, your empire. Although it may sound cliché, we really are living in a society where it has become more about who you know than what you know in many situations. In previous chapters, we already busted the myth that a degree can guarantee you success, right? It's simply not enough. Well, let me take that a step further and assert that submitting job applications alone are no longer enough.

At the time that I've written this chapter, we're almost 2 years into navigating a global pandemic/health crisis known as the coronavirus pandemic. This pandemic has changed everything from education, the workforce, to the entrepreneurship world as we've known it. Things have become increasingly more competitive when it comes to jobs in various industries, starting businesses, etc. Innovation, flexibility, agility, and willingness to learn have risen to the top as some of the most needed skills to maintain success. Those who are experiencing the greatest success in building their careers or business, or using their college education to advance themselves, are those who are stepping outside of their comfort zones to build authentic relationships through networking. Choosing to go to college, launch and grow a career in the workforce, or start a business, are life altering decisions. This entire time, I've preached to you that neither decision is a wrong decision per se, but the important thing is developing a strategy to make sure your choice yields a great return on investment.

How can you develop a solid strategy that will lead you to success? You guessed it, networking. Networking can help you gain new information that allows you to avoid common pitfalls, mistakes, and roadblocks that many before you have encountered when choosing between college versus career. It's through networking that you should connect with people who are currently doing things that you're interested in doing. For example, if you want to become a mechanical engineer, find someone who's doing that. With the internet at our fingertips, LinkedIn is only a search engine or app away from millions of professionals. Have a unique business idea? There are resources and people out there who can help you flesh out that idea, launch, and operate a profitable business, such as the U.S. Small Business Administration (SBA). Networking can even help you discover a mentor who can take you under their wing and guide you through exploring your academic, career, or business interests.

Believe it or not, multi-million-dollar empires begin with an idea and relationship building. After all, you can't learn every skill and you won't ever have all of the knowledge and wisdom in the world. There will always be someone who knows more than you, have been many more places than you, and have experienced more of life than you – they likely have a fair share of scars, failures, and successes to prove it. However, by taking the step right now, right where you are, to learn and practice the art of networking, you can begin to shape your path to success. You're not too young or too old to star stepping outside of the box to meet new people, ask questions, and seek out new information to determine what makes the most sense for your now and your future.

A few years ago, someone would be hard pressed to convince young me that networking had the power to change my life for the better. I maneuvered my journey to success with the mindset that hard work, dedication, perseverance, and resilience would get me far. Don't get me wrong, those attributes absolutely contribute to you getting far and accomplishing many things, but when I finally opened myself up to learning the art of networking and applying what I was learning, I began to see my life advance exponentially. Check this out...

In the last few months alone, I've landed several job interviews based on simple conversation and conducting what's called informational interviewing. I explain this concept in greater detail in the workbook I created as a companion to this book. In fact, I recently encountered an unexplainable networking experience that resulted in me landing a new job offer that almost doubled my salary. It all resulted from a simple conversation I had after connecting with someone in the technical recruiting industry on LinkedIn. The strategy that I cover in the workbook is what I used to influence such a positive networking result. Story time! After graduating with my MBA earlier this year, I embarked on this journey of exploring whether or not I'd reached a career crossroads and what was next for me.

It wasn't necessarily that I was unhappy in my current career – because I absolutely love working with young professionals pursuing STEM majors and careers; however, let's apply the principle we've been discussing – it's in my best interest to make sure my pursuit and attainment of an MBA yields a good return on investment. Now, while I was generally content with my career, I was ready for more. Hungry to experience what's next in my career with this new set of credentials. Yet, with extremely fierce competition in the job market resulting from the pandemic, casually applying for jobs online and tailoring several versions of my resume to each job posting wasn't working. It just wasn't yielding any results. Only rejection emails from companies telling me they decided not to move forward with my application.

After several months of this, I finally decided that I needed to "play the game" better. As I told you before, I was one of those people who didn't really feed into the idea of networking to its fullest capacity. Had I networked with others to build meaningful relationships in the past? Yes, but I had no serious strategy behind it when it came to my career. Shoot, I felt like with three college degrees and extensive work experience, I didn't "need" anyone to vouch for me. Would it be nice? Sure, but you could say it was a lack of confidence, or maybe even just feeling like I'm being a bother to complete strangers who likely wouldn't respond to my messages online.

Nevertheless, I took time to assess that my job search strategy was missing an important piece to the puzzle – relationship building which could result in tapping into the hidden job market. Pretty quickly, I got a bit creative with my networking strategy. I knew that I was someone working in higher education career services wanting to pivot into HR, specifically campus recruiting, technical recruiting or training and development. With this in mind, my networking strategy was two-fold: 1) Find and connect with as many professionals as possible working in the types of roles I was interested in pivoting into. 2) Narrow down my search to include professionals who had a similar background of experience that I have when they pivoted into said industries. For example, people who were former higher-education professionals now working in HR.

It didn't take me long to find dozens of these professionals on LinkedIn, and I also got creative and discovered relevant groups on Facebook dedicated to professionals leaving higher education. It was a literal gold mine. When I discovered each person on LinkedIn, I developed a habit of sending each of them personalized messages briefly explaining why I wanted to connect with them. Not only did I share that, but I was also bold enough to ask if they'd be interested in arranging 30-minutes to chat with me virtually about their experiences. I was shooting my shot. Sending those personalized messages was a part of the first rule to successful relationship building: building rapport. Establishing common ground with each person I reached out to helped me to immediately start showing value. Like I told you earlier, there are millions of users on LinkedIn. When you're in recruiting, you're likely to have hundreds of people sending connection requests and DMs whether they're looking for jobs, or, in my case, trying to learn more about what you do. I was just another person added to that.

Now, let me be clear in saying that when you shoot your shot in connecting with new people, especially online, it won't always result in receiving a response. Sometimes, your message will go into the abyss, and you won't hear anything back from a person you were so eager to connect with. That's okay! Take it with a grain of salt. That's why you have to focus on casting a wide, but strategic net when networking. Find and connect with several people doing what you're interested in doing. That way, if and when you decide to reach out and the response you get is unfavorable, you can just move on to focusing your efforts on others. That's exactly what I've done. Despite me connecting with dozens of people doing what I'm interested in doing, there are some of them who've yet to respond to my connection request and some who've accepted my request but haven't responded to my messages. For those who did respond to me, the majority of them were more than willing to set up a virtual chat with me to speak about their career experiences.

One of those people who were generous enough to make time to speak to me is what led to an interview that has changed my career. This particular person is a technical recruiter which means her entire job revolves around recruiting and hiring people interested in tech careers – software/web developers, engineers, coders, etc. We were able to schedule a 30-minute Zoom call, and once the time came, we sparked a conversation where she shared many gems about how she got into recruiting with a degree in

Finance. Her initial career goals were to work on Wall Street, but she got into HR after college instead. She then went on to share about the skills employers look for in recruiters as well as some of the challenges and successes she's encountered in the field so far. Within the first 15 minutes of chatting, she'd given me so much wisdom and insider insight into the industry that I was able to take and apply to my job search. Here's the kicker – I also used that conversation to tell her about my career story and why I was even interested in recruiting. I told her about my extensive career in tech and also working exclusively with tech and engineering majors as a higher education career services professional.

She was completely blown away at the experience I had, and she insisted that I could do well as a technical recruiter. At the end of the conversation, I asked if she'd be willing to review my resume and provide any feedback on how I could improve my content to better sell myself. She eagerly agreed, and I can't lie, I was pleasantly surprised that a complete stranger was willing to go out of their way to help me, even with something as minor as a resume review.
THE POWER OF NETWORKING AND GETTING OUTSIDE MY COMFORT ZONE! After our chat, I

immediately emailed my resume to her and profusely thanked her for taking the time to meet with me, sharing great advice, and offering to review my resume.

To be honest, I had low expectations of hearing from her again because of all of the reasons I mentioned above – she's a recruiter so she's very busy, she probably talks to tons of people every day so she may not even remember me, etc. These excuses were really thoughts that helped me to manage my expectations and not get my hopes up about anything. That's not something I recommend you do. When it comes to networking strategy, develop a habit of following up and staying in touch with new people you connect with to build that rapport and make yourself memorable. We talk about this in more detail in the associated workbook, so I've got you covered.

As we wrapped up our conversation, we agreed to reconnect in a few days once she had time to review my resume. Specifically, we spoke on a Friday, and she agreed to return my resume back with feedback early the following week. I vividly recall thinking to myself after the following Tuesday rolled by with no follow-up from her that I'd likely not hear from her again. I shrugged it off because I felt I'd already gotten valuable information from her, and the resume review would've been extra help. It honestly slipped to the back of my mind, and I let it go....until I actually heard from her later that week. Her follow-up email changed my life. In that email, she simply said, "I can do you one better. I've secured you an interview for the technical recruiter role with my manager."

Do you see what just happened here?! A simple informational interview led to me landing an interview directly with a hiring manager. This is the same company who had just rejected me TWICE for a similar role within a month's time. In a matter of minutes of email exchange, I had a 30-minute virtual interview scheduled with her manager for the next day. After meeting with him, he stated he was very impressed with my experience and my career story, and he felt like I'd be a great asset to the team; however, he wanted me to interview with another manager. That first interview led to another 30-minute interview with his co-manager three days later. I kid you not that I completed the second interview at 12 noon, and, by 4PM that same afternoon, I had a job offer for a fully remote technical recruiter position! Not just a technical recruiter role, but this job offer was a $40,000+ salary increase!

Did you catch the magnitude of that encounter? Intentional, strategic networking and stepping outside my comfort zone led to me tapping into the hidden job market and being referred directly for a job that I convinced myself for years I was unqualified for. We've been open with each other throughout the book so far, so let me be even more transparent here. A year prior, I was making about $34,000 per year. When I got my job as a career consultant, my salary increased to about $45,000 per year which was a good little bump in pay.

Within 9 months of being in that role, I received a promotion which increased my salary to a little above $53,000. Again, another good little bump in pay. The new job offer increased my total compensation to six figures, including over $50,000 in company stock and other financial incentives. ALL OF THIS AS A RESULT OF STRATEGIC NETWORKING! That's the power of networking. It has the potential to literally change your financial and tax bracket as well as your livelihood! I'd be lying if I said it was easy because it was absolutely not. I went through so many rejections, unanswered and ignored emails and messages from professionals I admired, applying for dozens of jobs over the course of several months and never hearing anything back.

My point in sharing those specific numbers is to help you understand that your net worth can be expanded greatly by being intentional about building and leaning into your network. There are many excuses that people use to limit their potential and keep them in a box – I'm too young, I'm still in high school or college, I don't have much work experience or none at all, they're more accomplished than me, they're intimidating, they won't have time for a nobody like me, etc. There's literally a million ways to reach your definition of success. You've just got to be willing to try new things and accept no's and detours as redirection while you keep trying and keep forging new relationships. You may not have the money or resources, but all you need is the right connection who has the finances, the resources, the additional connections, the knowledge, the experience, the _____ - fill in the blank with whatever you're lacking.

Connections are the core. Build intentional, reciprocal relationships that can yield the support you need to get to the next level. Make sure your intentions are pure and you're not out to be self-serving and selfish. As long as you're genuinely willing to learn, soak up information, and work smart, the quality of your connections can be your key to reaching your definition of success. As we wrap up this chapter on the power of networking, I want to share with you some practical tips you can begin applying to start developing or enhance your networking efforts even if you don't have access to the associated workbook. Remember, I got your back, so my knowledge is your knowledge, and my mistakes are your lessons learned! You've got your notes? Let's go....

1. *Start with Where You Are and What You Have*

The biggest misconception young professionals have about networking is that they are too young and have nothing of value to contribute when connecting with someone they're inspired by or are doing something they aspire to do in their future. Listen, wherever you are in your life right now as you read this book, be it in high school, college, a working adult, or entrepreneur, you're in the perfect place to start networking right now. One of the best ways to minimize faulty decision making on life-changing moves is by taking the time to learn new information and get healthy perspectives from others who've traveled the pathway(s) you're contemplating going down, be it college, building a successful career, or building businesses. Finding a mentor can be of greatest help, but I understand that not everyone has ready access to people in their immediate environment that can serve as such. I know I didn't when I was younger, so I get it.

Still, with the ease of access of the internet, you're only a few clicks or profiles away from connecting with someone who can help you explore and gain new insights for your path ahead. Of course, you've got to be smart and safe about using the internet and online networking. Nevertheless, if you're still in school, tap into the connections you have around you. For example, identify at least 3 teachers or professors you've had great experiences with. Approach them and let them know that you'd like to have a conversation about your future goals. Influential people respect grind, resilience, persistence, and determination. You may not have the highest GPA, be an all-around athlete, or whatever is popular to young people these days, but when you display the character, drive, and integrity, people are willing to help nurture that and guide you in the right direction.

Seek out a mentor if you don't have one already. If you're involved in sports, student organizations, or activities in your local community or church, observe your surroundings and identify at least one person whose actions inspire you to be better and dream bigger. Don't be afraid to approach that person. If you are in college, the resources are there for you to get more easily involved in networking opportunities. It doesn't matter if it's a community college or university, there are likely organizations, committees, and initiatives happening right on your campus that provides you with access to a network of professors, administrators, employers and recruiters, and even mentors.

From my time working in higher education, I've noticed a trend of more colleges developing mentor programs for current students across diverse populations. Often times, this is a collaboration effort with their alumni network who volunteer to connect with and serve students who are currently enrolled at the college. If you're unsure of where to start with discovering the various student organizations, departments, or programs that may exist on your campus, reach out to your guidance counselor (high school) or academic and/or career advisor (college). They are often the focal point to having access to other campus resources and opportunities to get involved and can point you in the right direction. You just have to be willing to ask questions and be relentless in your pursuit to find out what's available. It's okay that you don't know what you don't know, but don't stay in a place of ambiguity. ASK QUESTIONS!

Furthermore, everyone should have a LinkedIn profile that you're active on. Students, working professionals, and entrepreneurs alike! There's an audience there regardless of what your current title or focus is. If you're a student or professional, you can utilize LinkedIn to research employers and professionals by career titles or industry areas to begin building your connections. Remember, we discussed taking time to self-reflect on your "why." If you have an idea of what you'd like to be doing in the future but you're unsure of what it entails or what concrete steps you should take to move in that direction, start having conversations with people to discover what they do day in and day out, challenges they've faced in a specific career, and skills they feel have been important to ensuring their success in their chosen field.

You can also use LinkedIn to join groups dedicated to specific careers or knowledge areas – that's a plus because groups are where likeminded professionals aggregate, so finding a group dedicated to teachers or lawyers, for example, can help you get surrounded with a lot of people in one space. LinkedIn also has an "alumni" feature available on university and colleges' official pages where you can explore LinkedIn profiles of those who have attended specific schools or are currently enrolled. This is extremely helpful if you're in the stage of life where you're contemplating going to college and want to understand the experiences of others who are currently doing it or have graduated from a specific college. It's also just as helpful if you're already enrolled in a college and want to connect with alumni who majored in the major you're pursuing or considering. From there, you can connect with them and introduce yourself to spark conversation. These are all strategies and examples that I cover in-depth in the workbook, so go there to learn more.

As an entrepreneur, you can utilize LinkedIn to connect with companies, organizations, or professionals who are likely in need of your products or services. This will require you to have a defined brand and understanding of your target customers to make the most of your time on LinkedIn. You also have the benefit of creating a company page that you can link to your personal profile. Don't only focus on promoting your products or services to get sales, but also use the platform to give value to your audience through education, tips, strategies, resources, industry trends, asking questions, administering polls, etc. The neat thing about LinkedIn is that engagement increases visibility which means that people who aren't even your connections (yet) can potentially see and engage with your posts on their timeline based off of hashtags you use as well as based on your connections commenting and reacting to your posts.

I would be remiss if I didn't discuss a few ins and outs of in-person networking. As a student, you've likely discovered that many organizations host events where you can network with your peers, professors, and employers. Even in high school, there's often many things happening around the school whether it's related to sports – games, etc., or academic stuff. I want you to grasp how simple it is to start getting plugged in and creating networks that are lucrative for you. If you have access to a mobile device or laptop, you have the virtual social world at your fingertips. Start with what you have, and that's all you need! The rest will come as you continue to put yourself out there.

2. Be Authentic: No One is You & That is Your Power

The craze of social media in 2021 and beyond hinges on many people building an image or life on social media that's totally different from the life they're living in reality. You've likely heard of the phrase "fake it 'til you make it." That's become the go-to for many, even when it comes to networking or building a professional brand; however, I want to encourage you that authenticity MATTERS. Authenticity connects to integrity in that when you're empowered and confident to show up as your full self unapologetically, your integrity shines through even the toughest, most tempting situations. Another one of the most impactful quotes I've ever heard was while listening to the podcast, "Dreams in Drive." I still remember the particular episode very vividly because the celebrity guest was one of my favorite actresses – Jennifer Lewis. In conversation, the podcast host said, "No one is you and that is your power." Now, this was a few years ago when I first heard this quote, and I've heard it more frequently from others as the emphasis on authenticity in professional branding has increased drastically.

Friend, one of the best things you can do as you carve out your goals and dreams is to take ahold of that quote and let it lead you. I'll be the first to say that pressure is real in these social streets. What do I mean? It's easy to see others doing what you aspire to do at an astronomical level and it's like you're on the outside looking in wishing you could be doing the same or wondering what it's like to experience a certain lifestyle, level of success, all the popular connections, or influence. It's also common for many of those people to be faking it. Not everyone is as happy as they portray or have as much clout as they lead on. Many people sacrifice their authenticity to keep up a persona online and in-person, and you have no idea the stress, strife, and frustration they endure behind closed doors in meetings, in their work and personal lives, etc., while trying to keep up said persona.

Your biggest asset that you have is being authentic. Show up as your authentic self regardless of the arena you're in. Up until recently, you'd likely hear me saying, "be professional while doing it, etc." However, through deep understanding and education of diversity, equity, and inclusion, I've learned that the western (American) standard of professionalism can be rooted in ideologies and practices that are inherently non-inclusive. While that is a conversation for another book, the point I want to make is that as a part of showing up authentically when networking and connecting with new people, and even building your professional brand, think about your salient identities.

What identities hold true for you right now in your life? Some identities we associate with shame or embarrassment, such as being first-generation, having a low-income background, being a minority, being raised in a single parent household, etc.; however, those identities matter – they are a sign of resilience and triumph over some of life's most difficult battles that come with associating with said identities. Embracing and leading with your salient identities is important to being as authentic as possible when building new relationships.

The beauty about the quote I was discussing a few paragraphs above is that because no one is you, that is the strength and advantage you have in every space you go into. We're all unique and have impactful experiences that have shaped our outlook on life and the goals we set for ourselves. Because no one is you, your thoughts, expertise, perspective, and hopes for the future are powerful. You don't have to mimic your favorite social media influencer, your classmate, your friends, and not even your family.

Let's be clear that I'm not saying to become a rebel against anything or anyone who may inspire you, but your uniqueness is powerful enough for you to become a trailblazer in your own right, even with having people and things you're inspired by. Embrace your authenticity confidently as you introduce yourself to others, share your ideas, and take up space in this big, wide world. Your life story is powerful. Your why is compelling. Don't let intimidation of others' story cause you to dim your own light as insignificant or less than. The experiences you have were granted to you in order to use as fuel to help impact others, your community, and even the world if you allow it.

3. *Informational Interviewing is King*

I've mentioned informational interviewing a few times so far and how it can be a catalyst to successful networking and landing your next opportunity. I also cover it in great detail in the workbook along with examples and activities to help you build your confidence in setting up these opportunities. Informational interviewing is such an untapped gem. If you're not familiar with this, informational interviewing is simply the act of connecting with new people, setting up a brief meeting to ask them a series of questions about topics that are important to you. When it comes to career planning, the goal of informational interviewing should be to learn as much as you can about the person you speak with, what they do in their current role, what they enjoy most about their career, biggest challenges they've faced, inside insights into the industry, and any helpful advice they can share with you that may be helpful to you in your own decision making about your career goals and next step.

While informational interviewing isn't intended to be a challenging, intimidating experience, there is a science behind being successful in getting people to agree to meeting with you, especially as a stranger. If done effectively, informational interviewing can lead to job referrals, interview invitations, and ultimately job offers. On the other hand, if you're interested in entrepreneurship, informational interviewing can help you forge meaningful connections with key players and influencers in your desired market or industry. For many people, it can be intimidating and scary to just reach out to strangers you don't know and ask if they'd like to meet with you. As someone who used to be very shy and a woman of few words, I'm definitely not the type who "never meets a stranger." I don't mind striking up conversations with people, but it takes a bit of time for me to observe their actions and engagement before determining if they align with my current goals.

One thing I will say is, everyone loves talking about themselves. The way I see informational interviewing is inviting someone to a chat so they can brag on themselves. Think about it, who doesn't want to brag on themselves, their accomplishments, and what they know when given the opportunity to do so? WE ALL DO at some point in our lives! Informational interviewing is a great way to leverage this for your benefit. While not everyone will respond to your messages or emails or agree to an informational interview, there are plenty of people who will jump at the opportunity to give advice, brag on themselves and their accomplishments, and talk about how they've gotten to where they are with the success they've achieved.

I successfully used the informational interviewing technique to land my 6-figure job offer. I told you my story earlier. I connected with that technical recruiter via

LinkedIn. We didn't know each other prior to me sending her a connection request and then reaching out to her and introducing myself and extending an invitation for a virtual coffee chat. To be honest, I prefer using the phrase, "virtual coffee chat" instead of informational interview because, in my opinion, it resonates well with busy professionals. It reminds me of meeting up with someone for lunch over a cup of coffee at Starbucks. It's also a bit more laid back than just telling someone you want to interview them and ask them a million questions about what they do. Does that mean you can't call it informational interviewing? No, but my personal preference has been to refer to informational interviews as virtual coffee chats. It's definitely resulted in me getting more positive responses from the people I've reached out to in the past.

If you want to start taking advantage of the informational interviewing strategy as a part of building your network and getting into more rooms of opportunity, here are a few things you should incorporate to ensure you achieve the greatest return on your investment (of time, resources, attention, planning, scheduling, etc.) and that your results are as effective as possible:

1. *Establish your purpose or target.* Basically, what is your why for informational interviewing? What result(s) are you aiming to achieve? That can be getting more information about a specific career path or business idea, building your network with people doing what you're interested in doing, getting a job referral, getting and introduction to be connected with someone else that may not be within your network, etc. Informational interviewing will be nothing but a bunch of random conversations if it is not guided by a specific target or intended outcome.

I'm a very data driven, strategic thinker, so for me, having a defined target when I became more serious and intentional about informational interviewing helped me to clearly compare the outcomes of my conversations to what I actually wanted to happen. Among many things, I was able to effectively assess if I was asking the right questions to get better answers from others, if I was being as authentic as possible or holding myself back, if I was connecting with the right people, if the information I was getting was informative to the decisions I was facing, and if I was making the best use of my and their time.

Also, as a part of establishing your target is determining the frequency of your actions. How many new people will you connect with each week? Each month? How many informational interviews do you want to schedule and at what frequency? Weekly, monthly, quarterly, etc. I recommend no less than a weekly frequency. Moreover, what types of people do you want to connect with? Your goal should be to be as specific and granular as possible because being vague can have you all over the place. To help you narrow down the types of people you want to connect with, ask yourself, what specific career paths are you genuinely interested in.

Give yourself a limit of 3. That should help you identify the types of professionals based on the careers and roles they may have listed on their profile if you're using LinkedIn to search for them. Because I have an interest in human resources, specifically the areas of talent acquisition (recruiting), talent management, and training and development, this helped me to focus keenly on finding people on LinkedIn by searching for them based on those terms.

2. <u>*Develop a canned script (or email) that you can rinse and repeat for each new person you reach out to.*</u> What I mean by rinse and repeat is that you can use it over and over without having to rewrite a new email or direct

message for each person you connect with. You will, however, need to tweak your canned scripts in order to tailor to each person you reach out to, especially if you're targeted multiple career roles or business ideas. The script needs to align with the role of the person you're talking to which is even more of a reason to make sure you've defined your target before starting to send out messages. I provide example scripts that I use in my informational interviewing pursuits, including the script I sent to the person who agreed to a virtual coffee chat and was able to secure an interview for me with her boss ultimately leading to me getting my current job.

Your canned script used to communicate with someone you find on social media (ideally, LinkedIn) should include at least the following: brief introduction of yourself; why you're reaching out/how did you find them/why are you interested in connecting with them; one interesting thing about them you discovered from reading their profile that you both have in common (can be that you both graduated with a similar degree, went to the same school, have similar backgrounds, or simply you're interested in the role they currently hold); the invitation for a virtual informational interview (or coffee chat) to learn more about their background and current experience; a specific timeline (i.e. - within the next week); and a call to action – for example, " if you're interested in setting up a virtual chat, please let me know a few dates and times that work best for you in the coming week." Incorporating a call to action increases the likelihood that 1) the person will respond and 2) that they will agree to scheduling a meeting with you.

3. *Develop a bank of targeted questions you can use to help guide your meetings.* Once your acceptances start rolling in from different people you're targeting and you start to get confirmed meetings, you want to be as proactive as possible in planning what you want to talk about and how you will make the most of each other's time. Take time to intentionally reflect on what you want to know. Go back to the first step of defining your target. What is it you're aiming to accomplish? Use those thoughts to start documenting questions. Also, research common informational interview questions for _____. Fill in the blank with the specific role or business your conversation will focus on. Write down as many questions you can think of, but keep in mind you may not get to all of them so plan to pull 4-6 questions from the list for each conversation.

While you should prepare a list of questions for each interview you schedule, you should not rely solely on the questions to drive conversation because that would make it very mechanical and dry. You should plan to establish a direction with the first question and allow the conversation to flow naturally. This is the approach I take to every conversation I schedule, and it almost always ends up in the other person sharing a lot of nuggets of wisdom organically than would've been unveiled through the questions. The conversation should be natural and played by ear, not a call and response aka you ask one question, they answer it, then you move directly to the next question, and they answer it. This will challenge you to be an active listener from start to finish because the other person may bring up a detail or a point that you can expound on that may not be a part of the original list of questions you prepared. Ultimately, prepare well with questions but also be flexible enough to pivot based on how the conversation flows.

4. *Think about your career story, your interests, and your why, and prepare to share details about it.* This is a rapid way to build rapport and make the person more comfortable with the conversation. After all, they have made time in their schedule to speak to someone they don't

know, presumably. Building rapport can not only help them feel more comfortable during the conversation but can also be a way to potentially establish a foundation that could lead to eventual mentorship. When thinking about your career story and your why, try to correlate similarities between what you've researched already about the person you're meeting with. I mentioned some examples above of similarities that are common among professionals, but it can be anything that allows you to open up transparently as someone seeking advice and information.

I'd recommend framing the conversation by allowing the other person to take the lead on talking about themselves first. Invite them to share more about their current role and how they got into it. From there, weave in details about yourself and your experiences that are relevant to the conversation. The goal of sharing details about yourself is to ensure you're memorable to each person you're speaking with. Think about it, most professionals are extremely busy throughout the day and talk to several people. It's likely not the first time that someone has reached out to them for a brief chat to talk about their job. It's easy to cycle through conversations and float from meeting to meeting without retaining many details that would make people want to stay connected with someone they don't know. By sharing details about yourself to create common ground, you will likely intrigue the person and influence them to want to stay in touch, even if it's a follow-up email every so often to see how things are going. That is ideally the type of professional relationships you want to build. Ones that get stronger over time.

5. *Plan a call to action to end the conversation.* You should always aim to weave in a call to action at the end of each informational interview. The call to action should be aligned with all that was discussed, and if you effectively guided the conversation, it becomes easier to invite it into the conversation. For example, if you've spent time discussing your interest in a certain role and trying to break into it, your call to action at the end of the conversation can be asking the person if they'd be willing to take a brief look at your resume and provide any feedback on what you can improve or experience you can pursue to make you a better candidate. That's exactly what I've done in the majority of my virtual coffee chats, especially the one that resulted in my current job offer. Specifically, I asked if she'd be willing to take a look at my resume and let me know her thoughts from the perspective of a recruiter. I reassured her

it was no rush, but I would greatly appreciate any feedback that can help me get closer to my goal of becoming a recruiter.

She happily agreed to do so, and we both decided on a timeline for when I'd hear back from her. When the agreed upon date came, she reached out to let me know about the interview she was able to arrange on my behalf. 10x better than any resume review I could've ever gotten. It would've never happened had I ended that virtual chat without a call to action. Had I simply left it at, thank you for your time that's all the questions I have, I would've missed out on an experience that resulted in a job offer. Your call to action doesn't have to be requesting a resume review. It can be something simpler, such as setting up a follow-up chat after you've had time to reflect on the current meeting. That's another fantastic way to make yourself memorable. Again, the call to action should make sense based on the conversation you're having. Whatever the call to action is, make sure you follow through with it. This brings me to my last point about informational interviewing principles.

6. *<u>Follow up after each informational interview.</u>* I cannot stress enough the value of following up. At least a week after each informational interview, make it a point to follow

up with the person to share updates with them or just to share additional insights you've gained as a result of your conversation with them. It's especially important to follow-up if you left the conversation with a mutually agreed upon call to action. Following up can be as simple as sharing a relevant article that relates to what you spoke about, sharing an update on your activities since the conversation – if you've done additional career exploration, new insights you've discovered, details about progress made toward your goals (the original purpose of the informational interview).

Keeping in touch is a great way to reiterate that you appreciate the person's time taken to speak with you and you're serious about building a professional relationship. The worst thing you can do is ask someone for advice and not act on it in any way. Acting on it can mean simply reflecting on the advice and information received and weighing it against your goals. If you have conversations that create great rapport, this could be an opportunity to set up future standing check-ins with the person. That can be something you integrate into the follow-up – asking them if they'd be interested in checking in at least bi-weekly or once per month. While not everyone will have the bandwidth or flexibility to arrange a standing meeting, it will leave a lasting impact for them to hear from you. This intentionality is what often times leads to more referrals and willingness to connect you further to opportunities that may come up in their own network.

Wow… we've covered a lot in this chapter, friend. While the strategies and principles I've shared only scratch the surface of networking, I strongly believe that these are foundational steps to help you take the leap and build your confidence in the power of networking and its ability to help you reach your goals exponentially. The last thing I want to share as we wrap up this chapter and the book is a reminder that nothing happens overnight. Connections, referrals, interviews, job offers, etc. There will be plenty of ignored messages, no responses, things that come up at the last minute that force you to reschedule meetings, etc. It's life, and we're all human. The thing to remember is that all big accomplishments start with small, consistent actions. You must commit to showing up for yourself, being authentic, and pushing yourself outside of your comfort zone to experience the results you desire.

As I said earlier, it doesn't matter if you don't have the financial means, the resources, etc. within your grasp right now. As long as you're courageous enough to put yourself out there and build meaningful connections, you can gain access to the knowledge, resources, and financial support needed to propel your goals forward. If you need continuous support, you know I got you! Connect with me on LinkedIn at "**Kenyetta Nesbitt, MBA**," let me know you've read this book. I'll be cheering you on from the sidelines while also sharing strategy that is helpful as you build your network and your path to success! Let's turn the page together as we end this great dialogue on a high note…

It's Time to Eat Your Elephant

Ahhhh, it looks like we've reached the end of the book and the end of our time together....for now. I can imagine you're probably reflecting on the past chapters filled with advice, insight, strategy and information thinking, "wow, this is a lot." Maybe you're asking yourself or your parents, friends, or someone else – where do I even start with applying all of this? On the other hand, you may have read this thinking, "I know this, I know that, but how is this going to help me get to my goal of _____ (fill in the blank)." Anytime you undertake a major goal in life, whether it's strategizing to build a successful career, business, or even pursuing and obtaining a degree, it can feel like the destination is so far away. It can also feel like there's a million and one things you have to do to move the needle in the right direction. So many obstacles that stand between you getting what you want out of life.

No amount of success is achieved by making one big choice or one big action. Look at the people you consider to be an inspiration to you. Do you think they made it to where they are from making one big, bold execution? They just woke up one day, made a few decisions, and all their success appeared? Of course not. Major milestones, goal accomplishments, and success attained comes from a series of actions, big and small, that you commit to doing every day for however long it takes to accomplish your goals. You've read along as I've shared with you pieces of my ambitious journey to building my success – the highs and lows of being a full-time struggling college student while working full time, growing up in poverty with extremely limited access to resources, etc. You've listened as I've recounted the things that I've learned along the way and the strategies I've applied to help me accomplish one milestone after another , but I saved one important lesson for last.

You see, you can apply every single piece of advice and principle I've given in this book like clockwork, and things could still not go as planned. You will likely encounter some detours and setbacks. It bears the question, "What do I do when the going gets tough despite doing all the right things, setting a plan, being strategic about what I want, and building relationships with people who can help and guide me? What do I do when I've taken the advice given by trustworthy people who've crossed my path, but I still hit those rough patches where it seems like I'm working for nothing, and my goals seem to be moving further and further away?" I can't begin to count the number of times I found myself thinking those thoughts and experiencing those moments of despair and hopelessness. There was one saying I heard in college that has stuck with me through my pursuit of happiness and success to this day, and it's helped me to push through the delayed gratification and seasons of hard work and grinding.

My professor had assigned my class an extraordinarily complex, long research project that he knew would challenge everything we'd learned in our program so far and stretch our thinking about the world in which we live. He fully anticipated we'd have challenges, and we'd have to work to really earn the grade we wanted. As he stood in front of the class detailing his expectations, he wrapped up his spill by asking, "How do you eat an elephant…? ONE BITE AT A TIME." I didn't fully understand it then, but after all I've been through, the meaning of this popular saying becomes clearer every day. Think about the size of an elephant – they're huge, right? In the beginning, that research project seemed like a huge elephant that we were supposed to confront head on. But how? One bite at a time.

When you think about your success goals, I want you to envision and embrace that saying. As a big dreamer, your goals for your career and life are like an elephant – enormous, powerful, and, sometimes, intimidating. It can absolutely make you feel a bit unsure of where to start executing, what goal to start working on first, or what action to take first. Just like you'd metaphorically eat an elephant one bite at a time, you should focus on your big goals for your future by breaking them down into smaller SMART goals to tackle. Regardless of where you are in your journey – high school or college student, new or recent graduate, or a young professional working to become more established. When you break the big goals up into smaller goals, it's possible to lessen the overwhelm and increase your consistency toward completing each small milestone.

More than anything, I want to see you win, especially because when you win, someone else wins. There are people watching you, rooting for you, waiting for you to win. Their success is connected to your ability to achieve your own success because your wins will serve as a blueprint to help them blaze their own trail. Your people are waiting for you, and it is my hope that this book has provided you with at least a small portion of encouragement, guidance, and direction you need to feel inspired and equipped to carve out your path to your destiny. You were placed on this earth with a unique purpose to impact many people, and I can't wait to see all of the amazing things you accomplish as a result of betting on yourself and fully embracing being an exception to the rules. Cheers to taking it one day at a time, one decision at a time, one action at a time, one step at a time.

To Your Success!

www.ingramcontent.com/pod-product-compliance
Lightning Source LLC
Chambersburg PA
CBHW071700170426
43195CB00039B/2398